Lambs Among Wolves

By
Meade MacGuire

TEACH Services, Inc.
P U B L I S H I N G
www.TEACHServices.com • (800) 367-1844

Copyright © 2005 TEACH Services, Inc.
ISBN-13: 978-1-57258-332-0 (Paperback)
Library of Congress Control Number: 2005923542

TEACH Services, Inc.
P U B L I S H I N G
www.TEACHServices.com • (800) 367-1844

"Go your ways: behold, I send you forth as lambs among wolves."

—Luke 10:3.

Contents

Foreword

To be a genuine Christian means to be, in character and life, like Christ. Many who profess to be Christians and are members of a church show little difference in their lives from those who make no profession of religion. But one who, through the grace of Christ and the transforming power of the Holy Spirit, has become a real Christian reveals a striking contrast to those who are not true Christians.

The real Christian climbs the narrow path, with relatively few companions, toward the City of God. Kind, loving, unselfish, he follows His divine Master and fulfills God's purpose for him. One who is not a Christian travels the broad way, with the fellowship of the great throngs, who are interested in selfish pleasures and worldly ambitions and hold little regard for eternity.

With infinite love and mercy God is seeking in every land and among every nation to draw fallen human beings from darkness to light, from death to life. When through the influence of the Holy Spirit a soul is awakened to sense his sinful, lost condition and to long for salvation, with the peace and joy and victory that God promises, and turns from the broad downward road to the narrow upward path, he comes face to face with new and perplexing problems.

In this little book an attempt has been made to make plain and simple the answers to some of these problems. It has been written for the benefit of those who are earnestly longing and seeking to follow the Master, to develop a Christlike character, and to accomplish the work God has for them.

—M. M.

Chapter 1

The New Life

WHEN the temperance question was being agitated all over the United States, "turning over a new leaf" was a common expression. Many who were slaves to liquor or tobacco were urged to quit the practice, especially at the beginning of a new year. In fact there are people who still talk about it as regularly as January 1 comes around. The plan sounds rather simple, and many people are intrigued by it. They say, "I am going to turn over a new leaf and quit smoking and drinking." Many have tried it again and again, but they are forced to admit that it is not so simple as it sounds.

This expression was probably invented by the enemy himself. Every human being "turns over a new leaf" every night and starts off with a clean, unspotted page every morning. But within a few moments the page may be smeared and blotted with sin. Satan knows how helpless a sinful human being is to keep from sinning, and he is well satisfied with those who are forever turning over a new leaf and trying to be good.

What we need to understand is that our only hope is in obtaining a new *life*. The pages of our life's record will continue to be blotted with sin if we do not seek and find it. On this point no greater mistake can be made than to delay gaining this new life. According to the words of Jesus, when the door of probation closes forever, many will knock at the door and cry, "Lord, Lord, open to us,"

1

but He will answer, "I know you not." "Saddest of all words that ever fell on mortal ear are those words of doom, 'I know you not.'"[1] Every intelligent human being should place the matter of his eternal destiny above every other consideration so that the infinite sacrifice of Christ in his behalf may not be in vain.

When we have determined to obey the words of Jesus and seek "first the kingdom of God and his righteousness," the next great question is how to obtain the new life. In this matter we are to be earnest and prayerful, studying God's Word rather than accepting some pleasing human theories. The enemy does not care how many people think they are starting for heaven if they start in the wrong direction.

Concerning this latter point, I well remember an experience I had many years ago. After spending a few days with friends, I boarded the night train for home. About midnight I arrived at the junction where I was to change trains. I waited in the station for my train, which was due at three o'clock in the morning. I little noticed the many trains coming and going, as I was occupied with reading. At three o'clock a train rolled in, and I hurried out and climbed on board. Soon the conductor came and took my ticket. Looking down at me, he said, "Young man, this train is going back to the place where you bought your ticket." He signaled the train to stop at a little station, and I walked back three miles and waited for the next train for home. I learned that it is important to make sure one is going the right direction.

Meeting the Problems

For many years I traveled over the country, visiting churches, schools, and other institutions, and talking

---

1   Ellen G. White, *Christ's Object Lessons* (Washington D.C.: Review and Herald Publishing Association, 1941) 413.

with thousands of people. I appreciated having the young people talk with me freely about their problems and difficulties. One reason for my interest and sympathy toward the youth is the fact that I had some serious problems as a youth, which I have never forgotten.

One of these problems was my violent temper. I sometimes wondered whether anyone else had as bad a temper as mine. From early childhood my mother had told me Bible stories and explained the promises of a home in heaven to those who are good, and the awful doom of perdition to those who are bad. I never doubted a word of the Bible and early developed a deep desire to be a good boy and go to heaven.

But all my high ideals and desires did not seem to have any effect on my temper. When I went to church and heard a stirring sermon, I was troubled, especially when the preacher declared that we must gain the victory over our sins if we ever expect to enter heaven. Sometimes he mentioned such things as liquor drinking, tobacco, dishonesty, and a bad temper. I would be frightened and try harder than ever to get the victory, only to realize that my temper was steadily growing worse.

In my anxiety and longing for help, I sometimes asked older people what to do, and they told me I must *try harder*. Finally this made me angry, for I had tried as hard as I could. I felt resentful, for it seemed to me that if a Christian told a sinner he would have to stop committing a certain sin or be lost, he should be able to tell the man how to stop; otherwise it would only make him feel more discouraged and hopeless.

When I began traveling about and discussing these things with others, I found that many felt just as I did. They were trying hard to overcome their sins, but were compelled to admit that often they failed notwithstanding their earnest efforts to do right. As I studied the Bible,

3

I found statements which did not seem at all in harmony with the information I had been given. For instance, there was 1 Thessalonians 5:23, 24:

"And the very God of peace sanctify you wholly; and I pray God your whole spirit and soul and body be preserved blameless unto the coming of our Lord Jesus Christ. Faithful is he that calleth you, *who also will do it*."

I wanted my "spirit and soul and body" to "be preserved blameless unto the coming of our Lord Jesus Christ"; that was the goal I was striving so hard to reach, but here the apostle says that the God who calls me to that experience "will do it." Evidently I was trying to do what God proposed to do. In fact I was trying to do what only God could do. For years I studied this problem of how to gain the victory, and it finally awakened in my mind another basic question.

Why Do We Sin Anyway?

It has been said that "of all living creatures on the earth, man is the biggest fool." By way of illustration, if a wild animal is caught while young and has its paws burned a bit in a fire, it could be set free, but never as long as it lives would it approach a fire. But man—with all his wonderful intellect, knowledge, and reasoning powers—will sin and bring disease and suffering and misery upon himself; and then as soon as he recovers, he will go back to the same sin again. And he has been doing this for ages.

Has any human being in the world ever committed one sin that was a real blessing, help, and uplift to him? The Word of God says, "The wages of sin is death." This text compelled me to face the question resolutely and seek to find the answer to why men sin. When I got a clear, definite answer from the Bible, I felt that I had taken a big step toward the solution of the sin problem.

Our Nature Governs Our Life

Let us consider this statement of the Apostle Paul:

"Among whom also we all had our conversation in times past in the lusts of our flesh, fulfilling the desires of the flesh and of the mind; and were by nature the children of wrath, even as others." (Ephesians 2:3)

We understand that the expression "children of wrath" means that we are under the condemnation of the law of God, under the sentence of death, that we are born into the world with a fallen, sinful nature.

Adam and Eve were created in the image of God and were perfect physically, mentally, morally, and spiritually. They were pure and upright in mind and body, and it was as natural for them to love and obey God as it was to breathe. But when they yielded to temptation and disobeyed God, sin wrought a terrible change in their nature.

Every living thing has its own characteristic nature, and that nature controls or is the source of every thought and motive, every word and act. Had Adam and Eve retained their likeness to God, that divine nature, they would have transmitted that same nature to their children, and it would have been perfectly natural for them to do right in every thought and act.

But after the parents sinned, they could transmit to their children only their fallen, corrupt, degenerate nature. Since, as a result of sin, our first parents lost to a great extent the image of God, it was no longer possible for them to be pure and upright and obedient to Him.

5

We Cannot Change Our Nature

Everything God created, both in the animal and in the vegetable world, has its own peculiar nature, and neither animal nor plant can possibly change it. That this truth applies to human beings was illustrated by the Saviour when He said,

"Do men gather grapes of thorns, or figs of thistles? Even so every good tree bringeth forth good fruit; but a corrupt tree bringeth forth evil fruit. A good tree cannot bring forth evil fruit, neither can a corrupt tree bring forth good fruit." **(Matthew 7:16–18)**

Jesus was speaking about the condition of sinners. He meant that we human beings are "by nature the children of wrath," born with tendencies that cannot possibly enable us to be good and keep God's commandments. In our distaste for this condition we see a true Christian who has peace, joy, and victory. So we decide to be like that Christian, and we resolve and try and struggle; but our wrong thoughts, desires, and habits are stronger than all our resolutions. Then we see that there is only one possible way for us to be saved, and that is to have a different nature.

God's Wonderful Plan for Us

As the result of sin the image of God has been well-nigh obliterated from the human family, and man has been controlled by a fallen, sinful nature. God's plan for our salvation provides a way by which we may be entirely freed from this nature and have His divine nature restored within us.

It brings about a complete transformation in our lives and the restoration of His image in us. The Bible states,

"Whereby are given unto us exceeding great and precious promises: that by these ye might be *partakers of the divine nature*, having escaped the corruption that is in the world through lust." (2 Peter 1:4)

Our sharing in His nature is made even more personal in Weymouth's Translation:

"He has granted us His precious and wondrous promises, in order that through them you may, one and all, become sharers in the very nature of God, having completely escaped the corruption which exists in the world through earthly cravings."

With our degenerate nature it is not possible to resist temptation and cease from sinning; but when we are born again and completely yield to the control of the divine nature, the sure and never-changing promise of God to us is, "Sin shall not have dominion over you."

What Jesus Taught

It is plain that all our thoughts, motives, and actions spring from our nature; therefore we cannot live contrary to our nature. This nature every living creature inherits from its parents at birth. So Jesus tells us there is only one way to be saved from sin:

"Verily, verily, I say unto thee, Except a man be born again, he cannot see the kingdom of God." (John 3:3)

We are born physically when we come into the world, and life begins for us as human beings. The Saviour does not mean that we must be born again physically, of human parents, for that would in no way change our nature. But we know there is a natural, or physical, world and there is a supernatural, or spiritual, world. No human being has entered into the natural world since Adam and Eve were created except by physical birth. And

7

it is equally true that no one has entered the spiritual world since Adam and Eve fell except by spiritual birth. So Jesus said to Nicodemus,

"That which is born of the flesh is flesh; and that which is born of the Spirit is spirit." (John 3:6)

This spiritual birth is described in John 1: 13: "Which were born, not of blood, nor of the will of the flesh, nor of the will of man, but of God." Therefore, as we inherit our sinful nature from our human parents, so when we are born again, born of God, we inherit the divine nature. We cannot be the children of God unless we are born of God, and when we are born of God and inherit His divine nature, that nature will produce the same life and character in us that it did in Jesus when He was here on earth.

When all this became clear to me, I understood why I had made no progress while trying so hard to overcome my bad temper and other sinful habits and tendencies. I had been trying to make a fallen, corrupt, sinful nature do what only the divine nature can do. I could find no place in the Bible where God said I could be good if I would only *try* hard enough. But I did find statements which showed how mistaken that idea was. One of them was Jeremiah 13:23: "Can the Ethiopian change his skin, or the leopard his spots? then may ye also do good, that are accustomed to do evil."

Indeed, it is no more possible to make a sinful nature do right by trying, than to make a black skin white by trying. "Who can bring a clean thing out of an unclean? not one." Job 14:4. Our hope of salvation is not in our trying but in being born of God and inheriting His divine nature. An illustration may help us to realize this.

8

The Wolf and the Lamb

Here are two active youths who love to go camping in the rugged mountains and are spending their vacation that way. This morning they are climbing the mountain, over rocks and through brush and trees, when they hear a faint noise. It is a baby animal crying. After a brief search they locate the little creature, which is crying pitifully and appears nearly starved. They do not know just what it is, but feel sorry for it and take it home and feed it generously, and it soon begins to grow and become active. One day an old neighbor comes over and asks with astonishment, "Boys, where did you get that animal? Do you know what it is?" They are thrilled when he tells them that it is a genuine timber wolf. It grows rapidly and is playful, and the boys are proud of their discovery.

In the spring the young wolf is running out in the field, when he comes to a flock of sheep, with many lambs just about his size. He is fascinated and wishes he were one of them. Finally he decides that he will try to be a lamb. He imitates their actions, jumping about and playing with them and nibbling the green grass. After a time the sheep lie down in the shade of the trees, and a little later an old sheep opens her eyes and, looking at the young wolf, asks, "Who are you? What are you doing here?"

"Why," he replies, "I am one of the lambs."

"What! You a lamb?"

"Yes, I want to be one, and I am trying the best I can. I am doing just like the other lambs."

Do you think that little wolf would become a lamb if he tried hard? I know you will answer, "Certainly not." Yet many professed Christians say just about what the little wolf said, "I am trying to be a Christian, trying to do right, trying to overcome my sins; I am doing the best I can."

9

Is there any way that the little wolf could actually become a lamb? Perhaps you would unhesitatingly say, "No, that is impossible." But there really is a way. God could re-create the wolf and make it a lamb. This crude illustration pictures the only way any sinful human being can become a Christian, a child of God. We have inherited through our natural birth a sinful wolf nature. We cannot by any human effort change that nature. That is why Jesus said, "Ye must be born again." This changes our nature, and so the Word of God says:

"If any man be in Christ, he is a new creature: old things are passed away; behold, all things are become new." (2 Corinthians 5:17)

This "new creature" is a lamb, for the Lord calls all His children lambs, or sheep. (John 10:14) All others are wolves, for they are controlled by the fallen wolf nature; so when Jesus sent His disciples to preach the gospel, He said,

"Go your ways: behold, I send you forth as lambs among wolves." (Luke 10:3)

These vital truths are made plain in the following statement: "Jesus continued: 'That which is born of the flesh is flesh; and that which is born of the Spirit is spirit.' By nature the heart is evil, and 'who can bring a clean thing out of an unclean? not one.' (Job 14:4) No human invention can find a remedy for the sinning soul. 'The carnal mind is enmity against God: for it is not subject to the law of God, neither indeed can be.' 'Out of the heart proceed evil thoughts, murders, adulteries, fornications, thefts, false witness, blasphemies.' The fountain of the heart must be purified before the streams can become pure. He who is trying to reach heaven by his own works in keeping the law is attempting an impossibility. There is no hope for one who has merely a legal religion, a form of godliness. The Christian's life is not a modification or improvement of the old, but a transformation of nature. There is a death to self and sin, and a new life altogether."[1]

The Lord makes plain just what change must take place in our lives and the provision He has made to bring about this change.

"When the Spirit of God takes possession of the heart, it transforms the life. Sinful thoughts are put away, evil deeds are renounced; love, humility, and peace take the place of anger, envy, and strife. Joy takes the place of sadness, and the countenance reflects the light of heaven. No one sees the hand that lifts the burden, or beholds the light descend from the courts above. The blessing comes when by faith the soul surrenders itself to God. Then that power which no human eye can see creates a new being in the image of God."[2]

Again and again we are given the assurance of God's purpose to produce in us this transformation of nature and thus give us complete deliverance and victory over sin. Without this change of nature, all our efforts will end in failure and defeat.

"When the soul surrenders itself to Christ, a new power takes possession of the new heart. A change is wrought which man can never accomplish for himself. It is a supernatural work bridging a supernatural element into human nature."[3]

Genuine Experience

One of the gravest dangers we all face in this matter of salvation is the natural tendency to rejoice in a

1   Ellen G. White, *The Desire of Ages* (Mountain View: Pacific Press Publishing Association, 1940) 172.
2   Ibid., 173.
3   Ibid., 324.

11

knowledge of the theory of salvation, not realizing that it is not the theory of the new birth that saves us, but the actual experience. Let me illustrate: Suppose that one of the youth who has joined the church and is considered a "lamb" comes to the pastor for an interview. She says, "Pastor, I would like to ask you a question."

"All right. What is your problem?"

She hesitates and seems embarrassed, but finally says, "I am afraid to ask for fear you will laugh."

"Oh, no! I am interested in your welfare. I shall be glad to help you in any way that I can. You are a lamb, are you not?"

"Oh, yes; I was baptized and joined the church a year ago. I am trying the best I can. Well, the other day we were taking a ride in the country, and as I looked over in the pasture near the woods, I saw a dead horse. Do you really think it would be a sin if I should go over there and get a good dinner off that dead horse?"

The pastor looks at her in amazement and exclaims, "Why, my child, what in the world do you mean? You are just joking. Did you not say you were a lamb?"

"No, I am not joking; and of course I am a lamb; but lots of other young people are doing it, and I do not think it would hurt me."

"But is that not just what you used to do when you were a wolf?"

"Oh, yes; we used to have great times fighting over those dead animals."

Do you think that a person who, by the power of God in the new birth, has experienced the transformation from a wolf nature to a lamb nature would want to go right back and live like a wolf? How strange it is that so many professed lambs are always asking, Do you really think it would be a sin to do this or that? They are talking about the things they did before they professed to be Christians. I fear there are many who profess to be Christians, but they have not been born-again and are continually trying to make the wolf be a lamb. That is why the way seems hard and little progress is made.

Becoming Spiritual-Minded

Have you ever wondered why so many who profess to be Christians seem to have so little interest in spiritual things? They may attend religious services every week and practice the usual ceremonies day by day. But although they are full of interest and enthusiasm for many things, they seldom converse on religious subjects or mention them. Jesus said,

"Out of the abundance of the heart the mouth speaketh." (Matthew 12:34)

We like to talk about our friends, our sports and games, our hobbies, our social gatherings, our cherished possessions, and many other things which pertain wholly to this world. But how seldom do we get enthusiastic about our Saviour's love for us and our love for Him, about the wonderful joy and peace we find in fellowship with Him, and the glorious prospect of the future life with Him. Is not the reason for this clearly stated in Romans 8:5, 6: "For they that are after the flesh, do mind the things of the flesh; but they that are after the Spirit, the things of the Spirit. For to be carnally minded is death, but to be spiritually minded is life and peace."

By nature we have the carnal mind, but as we have noticed, when we are born again, we receive a new mind. The transformation of nature must take place in the mind. According to these words of Scripture, life and death are in the mind. Our daily life is a constant expression of what occupies our minds and, therefore, reveals whether we have experienced a real transformation of nature or have only a beautiful theory.

Facing the Test

Another lamb comes to the pastor with one of those questions so common to young people. This time it is about a book.

"Pastor, a friend brought me this book. She said that it is thrilling and that everyone who wants to be up to date should read it. Do you think it would be wrong for me to read it?"

The pastor looks the book over and finds that it is one of the popular novels which have created a sensation among novel readers. Then he asks, "Are you not one of the lambs?"

"Yes, sir. I am a member of the church and am trying to do right."

"Then I would like to ask you a question. Have you ever read your Bible through?"

"No, I have never finished it. I have started to read it through several times but never seem to get very far."

"Have you ever read the book *Steps to Christ* through?"

"No, I started that, too, but never finished it."

"What about *Messages to Young People*? Have you ever read that?"

"I borrowed one and read a few pages, but I had to return it, so I have not read it."

"I believe you said you were a lamb, did you not?"

"Yes, sir, I am trying to be, but you know one gets tired of green grass, green grass, all the time and wants a change."

"Strange," says the pastor. "I never before heard of a lamb getting tired of green grass and wanting to change to a dead horse."

How sad it is that so many who start out to be Christians do not understand the first step. They do not realize that the only way to become a child of God is to be born of God, and the evidence that they are born of God is a complete transformation of nature. The new nature produces a new life, a new existence altogether.

From the Old to the New

Here is another statement in which the Lord reveals the transformation that results from being born again:

"That ye put off concerning the former conversation the old man, which is corrupt according to the deceitful lusts; and be renewed in the spirit of your mind; and that ye put on the new man, which after God is created in righteousness and true holiness."
(Ephesians 4:22–24)

We are to *put off* the old man, which we have been calling the wolf nature, and put on the new man, which we have called the lamb nature. It would be an amazing thing to see a wolf re-created and made a lamb. There would be little resemblance between a cruel, vicious, ugly wolf and a gentle, innocent lamb. They would be unlike both in looks and actions. Let me illustrate:

The pastor and I are walking down the street of a city when we meet two young ladies, dressed in the height of fashion. We observe the artificial color of cheeks, lips, and fingernails, the gaudy adornment on hats and clothing. The jewelry and dress give evidence of more vanity than modesty. To my surprise they greet the pastor, and he returns a pleasant "Good morning." So I observe, "You seem to know those young ladies."

Lambs Among Wolves

"Yes, I have known them for some time."

"But surely they are not members of our church."

"The taller one is a member. The other one makes no profession of religion."

How strange, it seems, that I am not able to distinguish a lamb from a wolf when I meet them walking side by side! Do you suppose the Lord wants His lambs to look just as much like wolves as possible? The Bible says that sometimes Satan's agents will appear in "sheep's clothing," but inwardly they are ravening wolves. (Matthew 7:15)

I cannot believe the Lord is pleased and honored in having His lambs disguise themselves in wolves' clothing, by following the vain, or immodest, or ridiculous fashions of the world.

Having a Good Time

Many hear the ideals and standards of a true Christian life set forth and feel that they could not be content with such a life. They say they do not want to do anything really bad, but they like to have a good time—if they were to renounce their present pleasures, life would not be worth living. We can understand this when we think how unhappy a wolf would be trying to live like a lamb.

Imagine a wolf that is accustomed to prowling through the woods at night, killing and devouring innocent birds, rabbits, and perhaps a lamb. He is really enjoying himself—having a good time. The next day he is lying under the bushes, looking out on the green pasture where the lambs are playing in the sunshine and eating the green grass. Perhaps he is saying to himself, "How could I ever be satisfied with such a tame life? What pleasure could I have in trying to live like a lamb?"

16

Of course he would be right. Creatures of the night find little delight in sunshine; and grass would probably give a wolf acute indigestion. But if he were recreated and became a new creature—a real lamb—what pleasure would he then have in living the life of a wolf? No one can deny that a lamb has just as much pleasure and happiness as a wolf—but in a different way.

Some years ago I visited a well-known zoo, where I saw lions and elephants and many other animals. Suddenly I saw two large wolves in a pen. I watched them for some time, as I was thinking of them from the standpoint of wolves and lambs. They went to opposite ends of the pen.

One trotted east along the fence; the other trotted west. Of course they met when about halfway across the pen. Every time they met, each looked toward the other and gave a sharp, ugly, vicious snarl.

I said to myself, I never saw two lambs act like that; but I am sorry to say, I have seen some church members perform very much like those wolves. What a pity for a person to be so deceived as to manifest the spirit of a wolf while he professes to be a lamb! When a church member indulges in criticism and faultfinding, or manifests resentment toward anyone, is he not actually denying his profession? How tragic for one to become a member of the church and still remain a wolf!

"If any man among you seem to be religious, and bridleth not his tongue, but deceiveth his own heart, that man's religion is vain." **(James 1:26)**

Marrying a Wolf

Another matter which every child of God should consider seriously is his relationship to those not Christians. The Lord has given this instruction:

"Be ye not unequally yoked together with unbelievers: for what fellowship hath righteousness with unrighteousness? and what communion hath light with darkness? And what concord hath Christ with Belial? or what part hath he that believeth with an infidel?"
(2 Corinthians 6:14, 15)

How strange that many who call themselves Christians refuse to obey God's instruction! How strange that a lamb should even consider marrying a wolf! Just the mention of it suggests that the enemy is making every effort to deceive and ensnare the lambs in this vital matter. One who is a true lamb of God could not desire to unite his life with one of Satan's wolves.

If we have the nature of Christ, we shall love what He loved. We know that Jesus had joy and pleasure during His life in this world. So if Christ had a good time while here and found pleasure in His association with others, why should not we learn to find our happiness as He did?

"Enter ye in at the strait gate: for wide is the gate, and broad is the way, that leadeth to destruction, and many there be which go in thereat; because strait is the gate, and narrow is the way, which leadeth unto life, and few there be that find it. (Matthew 7:13, 14)

If we go down the broad way with worldly people, we shall seek the same selfish pleasures which attract them. But we must not think that because the way of life is narrow and strait, it has no pleasures. God's Word assures us that just the opposite is true:

"Thou wilt shew me the path of life: in thy presence is fulness of joy; at thy right hand there are pleasures for evermore."
(Psalm 16:11)

Deciding for Eternity

God has made us all free moral agents, and through all eternity we shall be what we have chosen to be while on earth. We may choose to remain as we came into the world, with our fallen Adam nature, and as wicked wolves be destroyed at last. Or we may choose to be born of God, partake of His divine nature, and develop characters that will entitle us to "follow the Lamb" as members of His redeemed flock through all eternity.

One night a little boy came to my church with his mother, heard this subject presented in the sermon; and then walked the long distance home. It was late, and the little fellow was tired. When he reached home, there was his father, who was not a Christian. Climbing up on his knee, he preached the sermon to him. His mother told me how astonished she was that he seemed to remember every point and that he brought them out quite clearly.

At last he finished. Looking up into his father's face, he said, "Now, Daddy, are you a wolf or a lamb? I know you are a wolf because you smoke cigarettes, and lambs don't smoke cigarettes." I have often hoped that that lesson brought conviction to the father and that the family will all be saved together.

How to Be Born Again

Let us notice again a few statements from the Bible and then consider how to be born again:

"By nature the children of wrath."

"The natural man receiveth not the things of the Spirit of God."

"Behold, I was shapen in iniquity; and in sin did my mother conceive me."

"Except a man be born again, he cannot see the kingdom of God."

"That which is born of the flesh is flesh; and that which is born of the Spirit is spirit."

"If any man be in Christ, he is a new creature: old things are passed away; behold, all things are become new."

I have been in heathen lands and have seen cruel, degraded savages transformed into kind, noble, unselfish Christian men and women. I have seen slaves to opium and other narcotics, and poor helpless drunkards, whose cases seemed utterly hopeless, open their hearts to the Saviour. By His divine power they triumphed over all their vices and evil habits.

This transformation is so amazing that some seem to think it must be something mysterious and difficult to understand. But that is not true. God's plan for helpless sinners, for whose redemption He made an infinite sacrifice, is simple. It would not be in harmony with His great love if He made the way difficult and perplexing to those He is eager to save. So He has made it plain and within the reach of all.

When I say that the way is plain and simple, I do not mean that it is easy and costs nothing. It costs everything. Jesus said, "Whosoever he be of you that forsaketh not all that he hath, he cannot be my disciple." Luke 14:33. The old "wolf" life must be entirely renounced and given up, and the new life in Christ must be appropriated by faith. Here is a simple statement of the new-birth experience:

"In like manner you are a sinner. You cannot atone for your past sins, you cannot change your heart and make yourself holy. But God promises to do all this for you through Christ. You believe that promise. You confess your sins, and give yourself to God. You will to serve

Him. Just as surely as you do this, God will fulfill His word to you. If you believe the promise,—believe that you are forgiven and cleansed,—God supplies the fact; you are made whole, just as Christ gave the paralytic power to walk when the man believed that he was healed. It is so if you believe it....Through this simple act of believing God, the Holy Spirit has begotten a new life in your heart. You are as a child born into the family of God, and He loves you as He loves His Son."[1]

Dangers to Avoid

We need to guard against two perils: One is the danger of thinking we must have some thrilling emotions along with the new birth, and then regarding the emotions as conclusive evidence of real conversion. We do not mean to imply that we can be born again without any emotions. On the contrary when we realize the awful nature of sin, we look upon it with fear and horror as we would a deadly poison. At the same time we have a growing love for and joy in God, who has provided a way of escape for us. But the emotions themselves are not the evidence of genuine conversion.

The second peril is that of being superficial. We may be sincere in confessing Christ and taking the first step, and then assume that "we have arrived" and nothing more is necessary. We need to remember that when we are born again, we are born spiritual babes, and certain conditions are necessary if we are to make normal, healthy spiritual growth into spiritual manhood and womanhood.

"The accession of members who have not been renewed in heart and reformed in life is a source of weakness to the church. This fact is often ignored. Some ministers and churches are so desirous of securing an increase of numbers that they do not bear faithful testimony

---

1   Ellen G. White, *Steps to Christ* (Mountain View: Pacific Press Publishing Association, 1956) 51, 52.

against unchristian habits and practices. Those who accept the truth are not taught that they cannot safely be worldlings in conduct while they are Christians in name. Heretofore they were Satan's subjects; henceforth they are to be subjects of Christ. Their life must testify to the change of leaders. Public opinion favors a profession of Christianity. Little self-denial or self-sacrifice is required in order to put on a form of godliness, and to have one's name enrolled upon the church book. Hence many join the church without first becoming united to Christ. In this Satan triumphs. Such converts are his most efficient agents. They serve as decoys to other souls. They are false lights, luring the unwary to perdition. It is in vain that men seek to make the Christian's path broad and pleasant for worldlings. God has not smoothed or widened the rugged narrow way. If we would enter into life, we must follow the same path which Jesus and His disciples trod,—the path of humility, self-denial, and sacrifice."[1]

There Is a Battle

Since we said that the goal is not reached by "trying," some might think that there is to be no struggle, no conflict, in the Christian life. This would be a serious mistake, for the Bible says, "Strive to enter in," "fight the good fight of faith," "resist the devil." The important thing is to understand where and how this conflict takes place.

Let us suppose that there are two brothers living in a country that is at war. One of the brothers is to remain in the capital city, which is an impregnable fortress. He is to fight from that position of advantage, to maintain freedom and victory. He can never be overcome so long as he obeys orders. The other brother goes out with a small army unit and is soon surrounded by the armies of the enemy. To have victory, he must overcome the

---

1   Ellen G. White, *Testimonies for the Church*, vol. 5 (Mountain View: Pacific Press Publishing Association, 1948) 172.

overwhelming forces of the enemy. These brothers are fighting from entirely different standpoints. One is placed in a victorious position, and his duty is to maintain the victory already won for him by his great commander. The other is struggling to overcome an enemy much stronger than he is. The first one represents the fight of faith of the Christian soldier. He is not struggling to overcome Satan, for that would be impossible for a human being. Jesus took our humanity and won the victory for us. He places us by His side in this victorious position and expects us, by faith and through union with Him, to make this victory ours day by day as we are assailed by the enemy.

"This is the victory that overcometh the world, even our faith."   **(1 John 5:4)**

Thus it is through constant surrender of the will to the indwelling Saviour that the divine nature controls, instead of our weak human nature. Every day the enemy will do his utmost to arouse the old nature and tempt us to yield to it again. So we see that it is in the realm of the will that the conflict takes place.

"Everything depends on the right action of the will."[1]

We cannot expect to make a success of the Christian life if it is just "one interest among many." Religion must be made the one great business of life. Everything else should be held subordinate to it. What other experience could come to a human being that would compare to the miracle of being "born of God" and becoming His child? Let us make sure that we have taken the first step, and keeping our eyes upon Jesus, let us cultivate the new nature which He implants within us. Beholding Him, we shall be changed into His image.

---

1   Ellen G. White, *Ministry of Healing* (Mountain View: Pacific Press Publishing Association, 1945) 176.

Lambs Among Wolves

Chapter 2

Love Is the Way

IN THESE tense days when everything is moving with great rapidity, we feel that we are constantly facing many serious problems. There are the financial, social, and educational problems, the moral and physical problems, the personal problems, and the family problems. What an array they make! And they all seem important. But let us remember that, after all, there is only one problem of supreme importance. Most of our problems are temporary and will be settled in a few days, or at most in a few years. But there is one problem which involves our eternal destiny. If we find the solution to that problem, we know that all the others are of minor importance and can be faced with courage and cheerfulness. The big problem is *sin*. Only that one thing can rob us of the joy and happiness of eternal life in the world to come.

Some years ago I was spending a week at one of our large denominational colleges. I was associated with a minister with whom I had not worked before, but I knew he was a successful evangelist. As he arose to address the students, his first words startled and rather shocked me. He said, "How many of you young people ever expect to sin again?" The room was quiet. I began to wonder what he could mean and whether or not he was rather fanatical. I waited almost breathlessly to hear how he would answer such a question.

His sermon was a revelation to me. It showed how little real study I had given to the subject, for the answer was simple and logical. Does not the Bible say, "Thou shalt call his name Jesus: for he shall save his people from their sins"? Now, how can He save you from your sins while you expect to keep right on sinning? We are saved by faith, but what evidence do you give of having faith if you ask Him to save you from your sins and then admit that you expect to keep right on sinning?

On the other hand if we pray earnestly in the morning that the Lord will abide in our hearts and will keep us from committing one sin all through the day; and if we earnestly co-operate with Him, we shall be giving Him a chance to keep us from sinning hour by hour. God is not going to compel us to stop, but He will save us if we follow His instruction. I speak of this because many have said to me, "Oh, well, everybody sins and always will sin as long as we are in this world. I never saw anyone who did not sin."

What Is Salvation From Sin?

It seems to me that this approach evades the question and ignores the plain teaching of the Word of God. How would it sound if I should say, "I accepted Jesus as my Saviour, and now I am a child of God. Before I joined the church, I was a habitual thief, stealing something every day. Now I try hard every day to overcome, but I cannot deny that I steal quite often." Would you believe in that kind of salvation?

I think of a man who attended an evangelistic meeting one night and was deeply impressed. He came forward and gave his heart to the Lord. After prayer with the ministers he went home happy. The next night he returned, but he had a despondent, almost hopeless look on his face. Asked how he got along that day, he replied that he had made a terrible failure and was sure there was no hope for him. He confessed that he was a wicked man and that he cursed and swore almost every sentence. He said, "I suppose I have sworn a thousand times today; there is no hope for a sinner like me."

But the evangelist gave him the precious promises of God's love for the worst of sinners and told him of God's power to save to the uttermost those who come to Him and surrender all. The man was encouraged and went home determined to be a real Christian. The next night he was at meeting again and looked quite happy. When asked about his experience that day, he said, "Oh, the Lord certainly helped me today, and I got along much better. I do not think I swore more than 500 times today." Would you call that salvation from sin?

I think of another man I met on the island of Celebes, in the East Indies. He had come out of the darkness of heathenism and was a member of the church. One evening in a meeting he was giving a thrilling testimony of the wonderful love of Jesus in saving him. The pastor whispered to me and said, "Look at that man. Until two years ago he was known all over this city and the surrounding country as the King of the Drunkards. But when he surrendered his life to the Saviour and by faith claimed His promises, he never tasted liquor again. One day one of his old friends came and urged him to go to the saloon and have a drink with him; but this man refused, saying, 'I have no desire for drink any more.' The man urged again, offering him a large sum of money if he would drink with him. But the man replied, 'Thank you, my friend, you keep your money, for I do not care for drink. I have something in here (placing his hand over his heart) which satisfies me far more than drink ever did:'"

If that man, a habitual drunkard, could be saved from drinking the very day he surrendered his life to Christ, why cannot we be saved from any other sin if we are really in earnest about it?

The more we consider this question, the more we shall realize that it is a serious one, and that we dare not ignore it. The Bible says, "He shall save his people from their sins." If I claim that I am one of His people and yet manifest a violent temper day by day, am I not actually and openly denying Christ? I say that I am His, but my life testifies to the fact that I am under the dominion of sin. I do not see how anyone can claim to be saved from any sin until he has stopped practicing that sin.

What the Bible Says

"We know that whosoever is born of God sinneth not."
(1 John 5:18)

There are many statements in God's Word like this which we read again and again but pass over lightly without much thought. We might be startled if we stopped to meditate upon them until their real significance is understood. This is especially true of statements in the First Epistle of John, which is sometimes called "The Book of Christian Certainties" because the words "We know" or their equivalent occur about 20 times in this short letter.

John the beloved disciple was well acquainted with Jesus and His teaching. After 50 years or more of actual experience in the practice of these truths, he wrote this precious book to emphasize those facts and principles, which every disciple should *know* as a practical experience. When he writes, "Whosoever is born of God sinneth not," we know that this is the word of God, and there is no place for the expression of our personal views or differences of opinion regarding it. Many do not want to face this statement without question and either pass it over lightly or declare that everyone sins. They do not believe it possible to cease wholly from sinning; therefore the text cannot mean what it says.

Keeping the Law

On the other hand, we hear these very people assert that we should keep the commandments of God, the moral law. They are scrupulous in the observance of the Sabbath of the Lord in obedience to the fourth commandment. They believe that those who have the light regarding the obligations of the moral law and still continue to transgress that law by desecrating God's holy Sabbath cannot expect to be saved. All this is unquestionably true, but why do they consider the transgression of the fourth commandment any worse than breaking some other precept of that law? Does not the Scripture say,

"For whosoever shall keep the whole law, and yet offend in one point, he is guilty of all"? (James 2:10)

Every sin men commit is a transgression of some precept of the law. I may be conscientious in obeying the fourth commandment, but if I disobey my parents or fail to be strictly honest, I am as guilty as one who breaks the Sabbath. How can I consistently and sincerely appeal to my neighbor to keep the Sabbath so that he can be saved, while I admit that I have sins in my life which I have not stopped and cannot stop?

If we all admit that God has made provision that His children shall have complete victory over all their sins, is it not imperative that we study to understand the plan by which this precious experience is to be attained and then co-operate fully with our Saviour?

God's Promises

"Whosoever abideth in him sinneth not: whosoever sinneth hath not seen him, neither known him."
(1 John 3:6)

29

"Whosoever is born of God doth not commit sin; for his seed remaineth in him: and he cannot sin, because he is born of God." **(1 John 3:9)**

"Whatsoever is born of God overcometh the world: and this is the victory that overcometh the world, even our faith." **(1 John 5 :4)**

"We know that whosoever is born of God sinneth not." **(1 John 5:18)**

"Christ came to make us 'partakers of the divine nature,' and His life declares that humanity, combined with divinity, does not commit sin."[1]

In view of these clear and emphatic statements, how can we deny that salvation from sin means to stop sinning? I know that many are saying, "No one knows how I long to stop sinning. I have resolved and struggled and prayed for years to get the victory over these besetting sins."

It is an important and necessary step in the life of victory to come to the place where we hate sin and long to be set free from its dominion. And it is imperative that we understand the means by which this experience is to be attained. How hard I tried in my youth to overcome habitual sins in my life! But I made little progress, and I was discouraged. It came as a surprise to me that I was not alone in this experience, for everywhere I went, I found earnest Christian people struggling with the same problem. I found them resolving to do better, waging a bitter struggle against sin, and—failing! And failing again! I was still more surprised when I discovered that the Apostle Paul had passed over the same road—resolving, promising, struggling—only to experience failure and defeat.

---

1   Ellen G. White, *Ministry of Healing*, 180.

"For that which I do I allow not; for what I would, that
do I not; but what I hate, that do I....For the good that I
would I do not: but the evil which I would not, that I
do....For I know that in me (that is, in my flesh,)
dwelleth no good thing: for to will is present with me;
but how to perform that which is good I find not."
(Romans 7:15, 19, 18)

Later on the apostle found the secret and cried out with
exuberant joy, "Nay, in all these things we are more than
conquerors through him that loved us." (Romans 8:37)
Oh, how I rejoiced when I learned the secret of victory
over that ungovernable temper, which had almost driven
me to despair! And how I longed to make it plain to others
who were having a similarly discouraging struggle! Now,
if we find by a more careful study of God's Word that our
failure has been due to the fact that we have tried to do
something ourselves that God does not ask us to do, and
which is impossible for us to do, we shall joyfully accept
the victory which Jesus has already won for us. Then we
can witness in our words and in our life that Jesus saves
His people from their sins.

What Is Sin?

"Whosoever committeth sin transgresseth also the
law: for sin is the transgression of the law."
(1 John 3:4)

Many are not interested in talking or thinking about
the law. They have been told that the law of Ten
Commandments was abolished at the cross, and we are
not now expected to keep the law. What a strange theory
for one who professes to believe in Jesus as his Saviour!
What are we to be saved from if it is not the guilt and
condemnation of sin? The Word of God says,

"For where no law is, there is no transgression."
(Romans 4: 15)

Others say, "I am not under the law, but under grace." What does it mean to be under grace? It means that by His grace you are united with Christ and have the experience of the Apostle Paul when he said, "Christ liveth in me." (Galatians 2:20) If Christ lives in you, He will live the same life He lived when here in the flesh. If anyone could be saved by grace, while ignoring and transgressing the law, then he would be saved *in* his sins. The Bible says, however, that Jesus saves His people *from* their sins.

The Secret of Obedience by Grace

We now come to the secret of the glorious experience of salvation from sins and the life of victory which Jesus has made possible for His children. There is one way pointed out clearly in the Bible by which we can obey the law and be delivered from the dominion of sin. The Apostle Paul gives us the key to this experience in Romans 13:10: "Love worketh no ill to his neighbour; therefore love is the fulfilling of the law."

One who fulfills the law renders perfect obedience. Jesus said He came not to destroy the law but to fulfill it, and that is the life He wants to live in His children. For years I longed for victory over my terrible temper; and I resolved, and promised, and prayed to overcome it, for I did not know at that time that the secret of victory was love. It does not say that love helps or enables us to fulfill the law, but "love is the fulfilling of the law." In other words love and sin cannot control at the same time, so to the extent that my life is filled with love, it is emptied of sin. If love inspires and dominates every motive and thought and act of my life, I shall be in perfect harmony with the law of God.

Love is the greatest thing in the world, for GOD IS LOVE. All the happiness we have in this life or shall have in the next springs from love. We long for love. Nothing else so profoundly affects our lives. Its effect is strikingly illustrated in a remarkable "love story" recorded in the Bible:

Jacob fled from home because his brother had threatened to take his life. He traveled his lonely way for days, past heathen villages and along the barren wilderness trails, a weary exile without friend or companion. One day he came to a well surrounded by flocks of sheep. Soon a young woman named Rachel came with her flock, and he learned that she was a relative of his beloved mother. He accompanied her home and soon asked for her hand in marriage. Her father stated the terms—seven years must he labor for her—and Jacob went to work.

We can picture this ardent young suitor, far from friends and his native land, lavishing all the pent-up affections of his lonely life upon the one most dear to him. Though the Oriental custom permitted no outward expression, yet love burned as an unquenchable fire in his heart as the days and weeks and months built up into years. Under the burning sun through the long days of summer, and through the dark, stormy nights of winter, he guarded the flocks and herds from robbers and beasts of prey, always toiling cheerfully, bravely, heroically, thinking of Rachel. The seven years seemed but a few days, because of the love he had for her.

As I pondered this story, I said to myself, Surely there is no one in this world so loving and lovable as Jesus. Is it not possible for me to know Him and love Him with a devotion that will bring every motive and word and act of my life under His influence, that will keep my affections so centered upon Him, that by beholding Him I shall be changed into the same image? Then I could go wherever He leads and bear every burden, every trial, hardship, danger, and serve Him devotedly year after year, and they would seem like a few days because I love Him so. And I would be keeping the law.

What Love Does

"Owe no man anything, but to love one another: for he that loveth another hath fulfilled the law."
(Romans 13:8)

Like many others, I once looked upon the law as being negative, a constant demand not to do certain things. Of course this dolorous approach pleases his Satanic Majesty, for he hates the law of God. As we study the Bible, we see how positively contrary that theory is to the truth. The law places a loving wall of protection around every child of God. If we loved God as He loves us, we would look with horror and loathing upon everything that He forbids in this law.

Some years ago I was holding meetings in a large city. One evening at the close of the sermon a woman came to talk with me about her husband. He was a businessman and a member of the church, but she felt that he was becoming so absorbed in his work that he was neglecting his Christian experience and gradually drifting away from the Lord. She requested me to visit him and see whether I could help him.

The next afternoon I called at his place of business. He was a friendly man and greeted me cordially, making me feel kindly toward him at once. After visiting with him a few moments, I mentioned my talk with his wife and her anxiety concerning him, and his attitude changed at once.

He began to tell me of the serious problems he had in his home, finally declaring that it was impossible for him to continue with his wife, and he did not intend to do so. I was very much distressed over the situation; and that evening, after the meeting, I asked them whether they would meet me the next afternoon. They agreed.

I earnestly hoped and prayed that after talking these matters over frankly, permitting each one to mention the difficulties which were causing trouble, they would acknowledge where they had been wrong, and the differences would be settled.

They came at the appointed time, and I asked the lady to present her view of the situation first. She did so, and then her husband stated his side of the question. I had hoped that as each point was presented and discussed kindly and frankly, the one at fault would recognize and acknowledge the wrong and make it right. But my concern increased moment by moment, as they seemed to get farther and farther apart. Finally in desperation I said to them, "My dear friends, I think your case is hopeless. If you would both confess your sins to God, and your faults to each other, and would ask for forgiveness, the Lord would pardon you, and you could go home reconciled and happy and live real Christian lives; but if you continue your present course, I see no hope for you."

They seemed to sense their serious situation, and we knelt to pray. I have never forgotten those prayers. The man wept and confessed his sins, humbly and earnestly praying God to forgive him and create in him a new heart; and God answered his prayer. Then his wife prayed, confessing her wrongs and pleading with God for a new heart. When we arose and they embraced each other, we were conscious of the presence of the Saviour. The room seemed filled with the atmosphere of heaven.

Some weeks later I visited their church, and after the service I asked the lady how they had been getting along since our little meeting. Her face lighted up, and she cried, "Oh, our home is the happiest home, and there is not a better husband in the world than my husband."

Then I found the man and asked him the same question and was thrilled by his reply. He said, "Our home is just a little heaven, and really my wife is an angel. There isn't a better wife in the world than she is."

"For he that loveth another hath fulfilled the law." It is heaven where God is because there all is love, and love is the fulfilling of the law. When our hearts are possessed with that love, it is heaven in our hearts, and thus heaven may begin in this life and may be in our home and our church.

Love Includes All

"For all the law is fulfilled in one word, even in this; Thou shalt love...' **(Galatians 5:14)**

There are 10 commands in the law of God. Let us glance at them briefly: "Thou shalt have no other gods before me....Thou shalt not make unto thee any graven image....Thou shalt not take the name of the Lord thy God in vain....Remember the Sabbath day, to keep it holy....Honour thy father and thy mother....Thou shalt not kill....Thou shalt not commit adultery....Thou shalt not steal....Thou shalt not bear false witness....Thou shalt not covet." All these 10 commands are embraced in the one word love. LOVE and nothing but love can meet the requirements of the Decalogue.

I was giving some studies in a college on this subject of love. One morning some members of the faculty were on the platform, and others were in the audience. Desiring to make a practical application of this truth for the benefit of the young people, I addressed a member of the faculty who, the students knew, regarded his wife with deep affection. I said, "Professor, may I ask you some questions for the benefit of these students?"

He answered, "Certainly."

Then I proceeded to say, "I understand there is a law forbidding you to kill your wife. Now, do you find that you must resolve, and promise, and struggle with all your power to control yourself and not kill your wife?"

He replied, "No, sir, I do not."

"There is also a law forbidding you to bear false witness against your wife. Do you not find that, notwithstanding all your efforts and resolutions, you occasionally lie about her?"

Again the positive reply, "No, sir."

"There is also a law forbidding you to steal from your wife. Really, do you not find it very difficult, and does it not require all your will power and effort to refrain from stealing from her?"

"No, sir, it does not."

"I am meeting people who say they want to be good Christians and are trying their best day by day, but in spite of all their efforts and resolutions, they fall into sin. You spoke as though you did not find it hard to obey the laws I mentioned. How do you account for this?"

Instantly the reply came, "I love my wife."

Is not that a simple illustration of the truth that "all the law is fulfilled in one word, even in this; Thou shalt love"?

And now let me state a principle which I believe is fundamental for every Christian: You never committed a sin against God in your life other than when you loved yourself more than you loved Him. And you never committed a sin against any human being other than when you loved yourself more than you did him.

"Self-idolatry:...lies at the foundation of all sin."[1]

---

1   Ellen G. White, *Gospel Workers*, 114.

If by the grace of God we deny, crucify, and dethrone SELF, and enthrone Jesus in our hearts, we have the victory over sin. If you really love a person as Jesus loves you, nothing could persuade you to kill him, or steal from him, or bear false witness against him. You would not covet what is his, but rather would always be wanting to give him something, for "love gives." Love is the source of all generosity, all sacrifice for others, all noble giving. "God so loved the world, that he gave." So if we love others more than self, we shall not sin against them.

Who that has struggled and prayed for years over this problem of sin will not rejoice to know that there is a way of deliverance and victory? That way is LOVE. Do you want that love? If you desire it more than anything else, you will seek until you find it. The promise is,

"He that seeketh findeth."   (Matthew 7:8)

Chapter 3

The Great Secret

WE HAVE been considering the fact that the key to the experience of victory over all sin, embracing complete obedience to the law of God, is LOVE. This victory gives us the assurance of eternal life in the kingdom of God. His Word says, "Blessed are they that do his commandments, that they may have right to the tree of life, and may enter in through the gates into the city." (Revelation 22:14) Jesus came to save His people from their sins and to give them eternal life. What many sincere souls are longing for is a clear explanation of the provision God has made for us to gain this experience.

"And this is life eternal, that they might know thee the only true God, and Jesus Christ, whom thou hast sent." (John 17:3)

Notice how beautifully these truths fit together to form an impregnable foundation for our faith and life. Why is it "life eternal" just to know God? Because if we know God, we shall love Him. We cannot really know Him and not love Him. And if we love Him, we shall obey Him. Jesus said, "If a man love me, he will keep my words." (John 14:23) Obedience is the real test of knowing God.

"And hereby we do know that we know him, if we keep his commandments. He that saith, I know him, and keepeth not his commandments, is a liar, and the truth is not in him." (1 John 2:3, 4)

39

Love is the fulfilling of the law, but we cannot love God unless we know Him; therefore knowing God is life eternal. There are many who sincerely desire and purpose to be Christians, but they do not know how to obtain that love, without which it is not possible to stop sinning. John, who was known as the beloved disciple, had much to say about love; and as we study his message, which was inspired by the Holy Spirit, we shall understand the wonderful provision God has made by which His true children may live in the heavenly atmosphere of love.

"Although there may be a tainted, corrupted atmosphere around us, we need not breathe its miasma, but may live in the pure air of heaven. We may close every door to impure imaginings and unholy thoughts by lifting the soul into the presence of God through sincere prayer. Those whose hearts are open to receive the support and blessing of God will walk in a holier atmosphere than that of earth, and will have constant communion with heaven."[1]

The Two Commandments

Those who are acquainted with the Bible know what we mean when we speak of the Ten Commandments, but probably many would not be sure when we speak of the Two Commandments. Let us look at the first one of the pair, the "old" commandment:

"Brethren, I write no new commandment unto you, but an old commandment which ye had from the beginning. The old commandment is the word which ye have heard from the beginning." (1 John 2:7)

A little farther on in his letter John makes plain just what the commandment is:

---

1   Ellen G. White, *Steps to Christ*, 99.

"For this is the message that ye heard from the beginning, that we should love one another." (1 John 3:11)

"And now I beseech thee, lady, not as though I wrote a new commandment unto thee, but that which we had from the beginning, that we love one another."
(2 John 1:5)

How easy it is to regard this command superficially, to say, "I love all my friends, and I do not really hate anyone." But there is a vast difference between not hating anyone and loving everyone.

If everyone in the world kept just this one commandment, there would not be a man, woman, or child on earth suffering today for lack of food, clothing, shelter. There is plenty for all, but some hoard up their millions, while others die of hunger and privation.

John states that this commandment came from the beginning. Let us go back a few thousand years and see how it was stated then:

"Thou shalt not avenge, nor bear any grudge against the children of thy people, but thou shalt love thy neighbour as thyself." (Leviticus 19:18)

As we read this, we may think of that dear neighbor who has always been so kind and has been such a help and inspiration to us. Sometimes when we have faced serious problems and hardly known which way to turn, this neighbor has insisted on sharing the burden and has given us relief and courage to press on. Of course we love him.

Then I think of a neighbor I had years ago. We lived just across the road from him, and for years he and his wife were pleasant and friendly, and we often did things to help each other. Finally his wife died, and he had our sincere sympathy and efforts to comfort and encourage him during this time of sorrow.

Lambs Among Wolves

I had to go for several months on a trip to the mission field, and soon after my departure my wife discovered that someone was coming into the yard during the night, emptying the gasoline barrel, stealing our garden tools and chicken feed. A friend came to help my wife, did some careful investigating, and discovered that it was our neighbor across the street who was doing the stealing. Do you suppose this old commandment, which says, "Thou shalt love thy neighbor as thyself," really means that God expected me to love that man as much as I love myself?

I confess it gave me something to think about, and more than that, as I studied God's Word, I realized that I must do much more than just think about it. Notice the words of the Apostle Paul:

"For all the law is fulfilled in one word, even in this; Thou shalt love thy neighbour as thyself."
(Galatians 5:14)

Here are the words of Jesus on the subject:

"Thou shalt love the Lord thy God with all thy heart, and with all thy soul, and with all thy mind. This is the first and great commandment. And the second is like unto it, Thou shalt love thy neighbour as thyself."
(Matthew 22:37, 38)

I do not wish to offend anyone, but I would like to put a frank, personal question to every reader: Do you really love anyone else in the world as much as you love yourself? Naturally we resent that question, for we are positive that we have dear ones whom we love even more than we love ourselves. But if we will analyze our conduct for a whole day, we may be astonished at our discoveries.

42

Loving Others

What would be involved in loving others as much as we love ourselves? We certainly would not quarrel with them, or criticize them, or neglect them, for we do not treat ourselves that way. Here again the Apostle Paul has given us some practical instructions:

"We then that are strong ought to bear the infirmities of the weak, and not to please ourselves. Let everyone of us please his neighbour for his good to edification. For even Christ pleased not himself; but, as it is written, the reproaches of them that reproached thee fell on me." (Romans 15:1–3)

Again let us ask ourselves a frank question. Have I done anything today to please myself? Have I done anything to please anyone but myself? When we meet a person who is constantly on the alert to do kind, unselfish, helpful things for others, not only for his friends but for all who are in need, we are impressed with the genuineness of his Christianity. He seems never to think about himself. He is following the pattern, for Jesus lived to bless others.

After considering these statements from the Bible, we may realize that if we are to measure up to this standard, it will require a decided change in our lives. And we may be more profoundly impressed, as we study further, to find that all we have studied thus far in this lesson has been Old Testament standards and comes far short of the standard for our day.

In 1 John 2:7 the apostle begins with the statement that he is writing no new commandment, but the old one which we have heard from the beginning. Then he continues:

"Again a new commandment I write unto you, which thing is true in him and in you: because the darkness is past, and the true light now shineth." (1 John 2:8)

In the Old Testament times the people were taught about God and His love by means of the sacrifices and offerings which pointed forward to the coming of the Messiah. God recognized their human limitations and did not expect such a full conception of His infinite love until they had seen it demonstrated in the death of His beloved Son on Calvary. "Now," John says, "the darkness is past, and the true light now shineth."

The world was flooded with divine, unfathomable love, when its Creator willingly went to the cross and laid down His life for poor, lost, degraded sinners. And Jesus gave this new commandment, the second of the Two Commandments, to His people a short time before He returned to heaven:

"A new commandment I give unto you, That ye love one another; as I have loved you, that ye also love one another." (John 13:34)

Let us consider for a moment the difference between what is called the old commandment and the new commandment which Christ gave His disciples. The first says, "Thou shalt love thy neighbour as thyself." The new command which the Saviour gave is, "Love one another, as I have loved you." If you love others as much as you love yourself, will you be loving them as Jesus loves you? In other words, do you love yourself as much as Jesus loves you? You can only love yourself with your weak, human love. Jesus loves you with divine, infinite love. See how He demonstrated His love:

"For when we were yet without strength, in due time Christ died for the ungodly. For scarcely for a righteous man will one die; yet peradventure for a

44

good man some would even dare to die. But God commendeth his love toward us, in that, while we were yet sinners, Christ died for us." (Romans 5:6-8)

We are thrilled when we read the account of a heroic sacrifice made by some man for his friend or companion. Nothing seems more sublime than for a man to lay down his life for his friend. Jesus said, "Ye have heard that it hath been said, Thou shalt love thy neighbour and hate thine enemy." (Matthew 5:43) This might be termed the human philosophy of all pagan times. But Jesus brings to His people an entirely new philosophy. His command is, "Love one another, as I have loved you."

When we remember that He laid down His life for His enemies as freely as for His friends, we must acknowledge that it is a new principle of love. He gave His life voluntarily for those who hated Him, cruelly tortured Him, and crucified Him. *Why?* Because He loved them and was bearing their sins so that they might escape eternal death.

Someone may say, "I do not believe it would be possible for me to love my enemies, those who hate me and persecute me." Their conclusion would be correct, for Jesus Himself said,

"Greater love hath no man than this, that a man lay down his life for his friends." (John 15:13)

How then is it possible for us to keep His new commandment?

God's Wonderful Provision

The question which naturally comes to us is, How can Jesus command me to love others as He loves me, when He Himself says that "greater love hath no man than this, that a man lay down his life for his friends"? May the

Holy Spirit enable us to grasp and appreciate one of the most wonderful and glorious provisions revealed in the great plan of salvation. We find it in the prayer of Jesus to His Father:

"And I have declared unto them thy name, and will declare it: that the love wherewith thou hast loved me may be in them, and I in them." (John 17:26)

How marvelous to think that our heavenly Father will take that divine, infinite love, which caused Him to give up His only-begotten Son to die an ignominious death on the cross to save sinners, and pour it into your heart and mine! Then we shall love not only our friends but also our enemies and all mankind with the very love with which God loves His Son. That is what God has planned and promised:

"The love of God is shed abroad in our hearts by the Holy Ghost which is given unto us." (Romans 5:5)

Now we may understand more clearly why John says he is writing a new commandment, "because the darkness is past and the true light now shineth." When that "true light" has shined in our hearts, we understand as we never have before that "God is love; and he that dwelleth in love, dwelleth in God, and God in him." Let us be sure that we have that light.

"He that saith he is in the light, and hateth his brother, is in darkness even until now. He that loveth his brother abideth in the light, and there is none occasion of stumbling in him. But he that hateth his brother is in darkness, and walketh in darkness, and knoweth not whither he goeth, because that darkness hath blinded his eyes." (1 John 2:9–11)

When, in answer to your earnest prayer, God pours His own love into your heart, you will understand more fully His word, "Owe no man anything, but to love one another: for he that loveth another hath fulfilled the law." (Romans 13:8) This is what the Lord Jesus was seeking to reveal when He brought to a climax that wonderful Sermon on the Mount:

"Ye have heard that it hath been said, Thou shalt love thy neighbour, and hate thine enemy. But I say unto you, Love your enemies, bless them that curse you, do good to them that hate you, and pray for them which despitefully use you, and persecute you. That ye may be the children of your Father which is in heaven."
(Matthew 5:43–45)

One evening at the close of a meeting in which I had lectured on this precious subject of love, a woman came to me with her face radiant with joy. She told me of the great change that God had wrought in her heart that night. Then she told me that about two years before, she and her beloved sister had been walking down the road in that village. The streets were covered with snow and ice. Another woman, driving carelessly down the street, struck her sister, and in a few hours she was dead. The shock was terrible for her. She could not rise above the feeling of hatred and resentment toward the woman who had killed her sister. The woman was at the funeral and came to her with outstretched hand, saying, "I am sorry," but she refused the hand, and said, "That does not give me back my sister."

The experience of those two years had been bitter, for she was lonely without her sister, and she finally realized that her hatred for that woman was robbing her of the peace and joy she had once known. As the beloved disciple said, she was in darkness and knew not where she was going.

But that night God had caused the darkness to pass and the true light to shine in her heart. She said, "Tonight I have seen the situation as it is. I know I can never be saved with that bitter resentment and hatred in my heart, and I would forever be separated from my dear sister. But I have cried earnestly to the Lord to take that hatred all away and fill me with His own love. Oh, how happy I am to tell you that God has forgiven me! I love that woman. I am going at once to tell her how sorry I am for the way I treated her, and ask her to forgive me. I want her to be saved."

Do you not think that was love from the heart of God? Jesus said,

"By this shall all men know that ye are my disciples, if ye have love one to another." **(John 13:35)**

Chapter 4

Are You Dead or Alive?

THE QUESTION posed in the chapter title may seem like a strange one unless it has been studied from the standpoint of God's Word. Many may be amazed to learn that millions who think they are very much alive are really dead. Let us go back to the record of creation and get a better understanding of what it means to be alive or dead.

> "The Lord God planted a garden eastward in Eden; and there he put the man whom he had formed." "And the Lord God commanded the man, saying, Of every tree of the garden thou mayest freely eat: but of the tree of the knowledge of good and evil, thou shalt not eat of it; for in the day that thou eatest thereof thou shalt surely die." (Genesis 2:8, 16, 17)

For a long time this text created a perplexing problem for me. Adam and Eve ate of the fruit of that forbidden tree, but they continued to live for hundreds of years. However, I found that the solution was simple when I studied other statements in the Bible. For example, 1 Timothy 5:6 states, "But she that liveth in pleasure is dead while she liveth." Thus it is clear that the Bible makes a distinction between physical life and spiritual life.

God is the source of all life, and at creation He endowed all the creatures He had made with physical life. He then created Adam and Eve "in his own image," and He endowed men with intellectual and spiritual faculties which placed them on a plane far above all other living creatures on earth. They were created in His image—pure, holy, and endowed with eternal life; but it was theirs only as long as they were obedient and loyal to their Creator.

By way of illustration, imagine two invisible lines coming down from God to this world. One conveys physical or animal life to every living creature. Over the other lines comes spiritual or eternal life, which makes it possible for man to live a holy, happy life forever. But man is warned that if he chooses to disobey God, the spiritual lifeline will be instantly severed, and he will be dead spiritually, though alive physically. This is what occurred to Adam and Eve the moment they disobeyed God. They lived on physically, but were dead spiritually until God revealed His wonderful plan of salvation through the sacrifice of His beloved Son, who was to bear the death penalty to save man.

The Bible tells us plainly that "death passed upon all men, for that all have sinned." Romans 5:12. The sentence of death was passed upon the human race when Adam and Eve sinned, but God had a plan by which every member of the race could have another chance.

"For God so loved the world, that he gave his only begotten Son, that whosoever believeth in him should not perish, but have everlasting life." (John 3:16)

Millions of human beings go about their activities day by day, physically alive the same as other animals, and not realizing that they are dead from the standpoint of eternal life. How shocking it is to think that probably the great majority of the people we meet on the street are dead! And it is sad indeed to think that this also may apply to many who regard themselves as Christians.

**"I know your doings—you are supposed to be alive, but
in reality you are dead. Rouse yourself and keep
awake, and strengthen those things which remain but
have well-nigh perished; for I have found no doings of
yours free from imperfection in the sight of My God."**
(Revelation 3:2, 3, Weymouth's Translation)

How important it is that we understand what really
takes place when we are born again and become real
children of God!

**"And you hath he quickened, who were dead in
trespasses and sins."** **(Ephesians 2:1)**

**"Neither yield ye your members, as instruments of
unrighteousness unto sin; but yield yourselves unto
God, as those that are alive from the dead, and your
members as instruments of righteousness unto God."**
(Romans 6:13)

We can hardly think of any miracle more amazing than
to stand beside a casket containing the body of some loved
one and see that person resurrected and filled with life
and energy again. Should not our hearts be deeply stirred
when we realize that we were dead spiritually and that
because of His infinite love and mercy the almighty
Life-giver has raised us from the dead, and we have
eternal life?

**"But God, who is rich in mercy, for his great love
wherewith he loved us, even when we were dead in
sins, hath quickened us together with Christ."**
(Ephesians 2:4, 5)

It was because of His great love wherewith He loved us
that He raised us from the dead.

**"Yea, I have loved thee with an everlasting love; there-
fore with loving kindness have I drawn thee."**
(Jeremiah 31:3)

Do You Know You Are Alive?

It is evident that many are not aware of the fact that they are dead. How could any intelligent being who has any true conception of the importance of eternal life be content with mere physical life? How earnestly we should seek to meet the conditions which our loving heavenly Father offers to raise us from the dead and give us eternal life!

"We know that we have passed from death unto life because we love the brethren." (1 John 3:14)

"As for us, we know that we have already passed out of death into Life—because we love our brother men." (1 John 3:14, Weymouth's Translation)

Here we have God's test by which we may determine whether we are dead or alive. And now we can understand the statement, "She that liveth in pleasure is dead while she liveth." She loves herself and lives to please and enjoy herself, thinking only of her own desires and pleasures—and she is dead spiritually. Jesus lived to bless others, and so do all whom He has raised from the dead.

Since this is the divinely given test which proves whether we are dead or alive, would it not be well to give earnest study to this matter of love for others? The Bible says, "He who is destitute of love continues dead." (1 John 3:14, Weymouth's Translation) We have already noticed how clearly the Bible teaches that "love is the fulfilling of the law"; therefore if we are saved from all our sins and are living victorious lives, it will be because we have been raised from the dead and God has shed abroad His love in our hearts. Then we shall love our fellow men as God loves us.

"Beloved, let us love one another: for love is of God; and everyone that loveth is born of God, and knoweth God. He that loveth not knoweth not God; for God is love. In this was manifested the love of God toward us, because that God sent his only begotten Son into the world, that we might live through him." (1 John 4:7-9)

Here again we notice that love is the test of the new birth, for when we are born of God, we inherit His divine nature; and since God is *love*, wherever His nature controls, love will reign. On the other hand, if love does not reign in our lives, it is proof that we have not been born again, proof that we do not know God, proof that we abide "in death."

Our Relation to God

It is in this epistle written by the "beloved disciple" that we have a wonderful revelation of the union and fellowship that is to exist between God and His earthly children. We are told that *God* is love. This would include the Father, the Son, and the Holy Spirit, the three living persons in the heavenly trio.

"And we have known and believed the love that God hath to us. God is love; and he that dwelleth in love dwelleth in God, and God in him." (1 John 4:16)

It is a wonderful thing to experience genuine repentance for all our sins, to be born again, and to unite with the church. Then, as we follow on to know the Lord, we shall have an ever increasing consciousness of our living union with God; we abide in Him, and He in us, and we are surrounded with His presence. How the aged disciple loved to dwell on this subject!

"No man hath seen God at any time. If we love one another, God dwelleth in us, and his love is perfected in us." (1 John 4:12)

"Whosoever shall confess that Jesus is the Son of God, God dwelleth in him, and he in God."   (1 John 4:15)

The Effect of Love

As we study these precious truths, we are thrilled with the fact that love makes us perfectly obedient to the will of God. "Love is the fulfilling of the law." If we are controlled by His love, we shall avoid doing anything that would displease or grieve our heavenly Father or doing anything to wrong our fellow men. The Holy Spirit will abide in us; and "the fruit of the Spirit is love, joy, peace, longsuffering, gentleness, goodness, faith, meekness, temperance."

We are living in the last days of this world's history, the time when, we are told, "the devil is come down unto you, having great wrath, because he knoweth that he hath but a short time." We see on every hand the increasing results of his supernatural power, driving men to crime and warfare. We see calamities, accidents, and disasters on every hand. The Saviour, looking forward to this time, tells of the effect these conditions will have upon the people:

"Men's hearts failing them for fear, and for looking after those things which are coming on the earth."
(Luke 21:26)

And then we see how His great love makes provision for His children in this time of trouble:

"Love has in it no element of fear; but perfect love drives away fear, because fear involves pain, and if a man gives way to fear, there is something imperfect in his love."   (1 John 4:18, Weymouth's Translation)

This is not just a beautiful theory, but a wonderful experience to those who have claimed the promise by faith. I have been in heathen lands and with other missionaries have had savages, bandits, and fanatics blazing away at us with their guns. Despite the bullets flying around us, we felt no more fear than when we were resting in our homes. Why should we fear when we have the assurance of being surrounded with His almighty presence? In a raging storm on the ocean in a small boat, or in an airplane far up in the clouds in a storm, what could be more restful and comforting than the knowledge that we are sheltered in the hollow of His almighty hand?

We think of John as the great teacher of love, but the Apostle Paul also gives us most precious lessons on this subject. How much his earnest prayer should mean to every child of God!

"For this cause I bow my knees unto the Father of our Lord Jesus Christ, of whom the whole family in heaven and earth is named, that he would grant you, according to the riches of his glory, to be strengthened with might by his Spirit in the inner man; that Christ may dwell in your hearts by faith; that ye, being rooted and grounded in love, may be able to comprehend with all saints what is the breadth, and length, and depth, and height; and to know the love of Christ, which passeth knowledge, that ye might be filled with all the fulness of God." (Ephesians 3:14–19)

How trifling and unimportant are all the ambitions and aspirations of the pleasure lover, the one who is dead to eternal things, in comparison with the ideals here set before us!

What Is Delaying the Coming of Jesus?

In His messages to the seven churches, which cover seven periods of time from the days of the apostle until the close of probation, the Lord in the Book of Revelation gives a special message to the remnant church. To several of the churches He gives solemn reproof and warnings because of heresy and false teaching. But there is no suggestion that the remnant church is teaching anything but the pure gospel of Christ. However, there is decided reproof because of the spiritual condition of its members. He says they are "lukewarm, and neither cold nor hot." They say they are rich and increased with goods, and have need of nothing, while they are actually wretched, and miserable, and poor, and blind, and naked, and know it not. In His great love and mercy He points out the cause of their failure and tells them the remedy:

"I counsel thee to buy of me gold tried in the fire, that thou mayest be rich; and white raiment, that thou mayest be clothed, and that the shame of thy nakedness do not appear; and anoint thine eyes with eyesalve, that thou mayest see. As many as I love, I rebuke and chasten; be zealous therefore, and repent." (Revelation 3:17–19)

In their sad and deplorable condition of spiritual poverty and wretchedness, the first and greatest need is for "gold," which means LOVE and FAITH. And so we are told that "lack of love and faith are the great sins of which God's people are now guilty."

In view of all this precious instruction the Lord has given us about the importance of love, and the fact that our lack of love is delaying His coming, how can we refrain from bowing humbly before our merciful heavenly Father and entreating Him to pour His own divine love into our poor, starved hearts? Let us not rest until it overflows in streams of living water to those about us who are still dead.

The Importance of Love

And now, before leaving this wonderful subject of love, which helps us to understand much more fully what it means to be alive and to be real Christians, let us notice how utterly worthless is a profession of Christianity if we are not filled with the love of God. We shall look at Paul's message, using Weymouth's Translation:

"If I can speak with the tongues of men and of angels, but am destitute of Love, I have but become a loud-sounding trumpet or a clanging cymbal."
(1 Corinthians 13:1)

Think how thrilling it would be to be able to speak with the voice of an angel from heaven! All the education and training of the greatest worldly institutions would not enable us to do that. Yet without love all our beautiful oratory would be as worthless as a clanging cymbal.

"If I possess the of prophecy and am versed in all mysteries and all knowledge, and have such absolute faith that I can remove mountains, but am destitute of love, I am nothing." **(1 Corinthians 13:2)**

Think what it would mean to possess the gift of prophecy and be able to foretell future events! And think what we could do if we understood *all* mysteries and *all* knowledge! These illustrations are evidently used to reveal to us the comparative worthlessness of the things men prize so highly, apart from love. And why should it not be so when we realize that "he that loveth not knoweth not God; for God is love"? (1 John 4:8)

"He that loveth not his brother abideth in death."
(1 John 3:14)

And now, after looking at the nothingness of life without love, we are shown the wonderful beauty and attractions of a life of love:

"Love is patient and kind. Love knows neither envy nor jealousy. Love is not forward and self-assertive, nor boastful and conceited. She does not behave herself unbecomingly, nor seeks to aggrandize herself,

nor blaze out in passionate anger, nor brood over
wrongs. She finds no pleasure in injustice done to
others, but joyfully sides with the truth. She knows
how to be silent. She is full of trust, full of hope, full of
patient endurance. Love never fails."
(1 Corinthians 13:4–8, Weymouth's Translation)

Let us come back for a moment to that inspired statement of how we may know whether we are alive or dead:

"As for us, we know that we have already passed out of
death into Life— because we love our brother men. He
who is destitute of love continues dead."
(1 John 3:14, Weymouth's Translation)

Would we not be wise to ask ourselves the question,
How concerned do I feel day by day as I meet precious
souls for whom Christ gave His life, who are dead and do
not realize it? We know the provision God has made to
raise them to life-eternal life. We may think that they are
not interested, but would it not be worthwhile to make an
earnest effort to awaken their interest? We have read in
the Word of God that if we do not love them, we are still
dead. Are we not making a tragic mistake to assume that
we have eternal life if the love of God does not fill our
hearts and overflow in streams of living water as we seek
to win lost souls to the Life-giver?

"By this shall all men know that ye are my disciples, if
ye have love one to another."   (John 13:35)

Chapter 5

Victory by Dying, Not by Trying

IN OUR former study we noticed from the Bible that Adam and Eve were created in the image of God, with a pure, upright, sinless nature. But through disobedience our first parents became fallen, impure, corrupt, and incapable of doing right. Then God, in His great love and mercy, revealed to Adam that He had provided a plan to give man another chance.

That plan would necessarily include the restoration of his nature from the fallen, degenerate state to its original purity and uprightness, or, as we studied before, from the wolf nature to a lamb nature. And let us keep in mind that it is the Lamb of God, which taketh away the sin of the world, whose nature is to be restored in His people.

It is important to understand just how God plans to accomplish this transformation of nature in order that we may co-operate with Him. Many say that the way is simple and easy, for all that is necessary is to "believe on the Lord Jesus Christ" and we shall be saved.

Those who try this—with an earnest, sincere determination to put away all their sins and evil habits and develop a character like that of the Master—find that they are engaged in a conflict with an enemy more powerful than they are. They cannot stop sinning while controlled by a sinful nature, and they cannot change their nature by trying. Let us notice what is involved in God's plan to transform our natures:

"Then said Jesus unto his disciples, If any man will come after me, let him deny himself, and take up his cross, and follow me. For whosoever will save his life shall lose it; and whosoever will lose his life for my sake shall find it." (Matthew 16:24, 25)

"And he said to them all, If any man will come after me, let him deny himself, and take up his cross daily, and follow me." (Luke 9:23)

Let us look at the setting in which these words were spoken; it may help us to grasp their meaning more fully. In the days when Jesus was here on earth, the Roman government punished certain types of criminals with crucifixion. Just outside the gates of Roman prisons there were small alcoves where crosses were kept. Probably more than once the disciples had watched the soldiers as they led a man out through the gate of a prison and commanded him to take a cross up on his shoulders.

Perhaps such a scene was being enacted at this very moment, and the man was being led down the street bearing his cross. The people stop to watch the tragic scene, knowing that in a few moments this man would be hanging helpless on the cross. Quietly the disciples stand about the Master, when He makes the statement, "If any man will come after me, let him deny himself, and take up his cross, and follow me."

Shocked and perplexed at this strange announcement, one of the disciples says, "But, Master, that man is going out beyond the city gate, to die on that cross."

And Jesus might reply: "That man has transgressed the Roman laws and is under the sentence of death. He is going out under compulsion, to be crucified and die physically. Every man in this world has transgressed the divine law of God, and so death hath passed upon all men. But there is one way to escape that eternal death.

"I have come to this world to redeem the fallen race, by bearing all their penalty on the cross. If any man will come and follow Me and give himself wholly to Me, his sins will be forgiven, and My righteousness will be placed to his credit. But something more than pardon must take place before he can enter the kingdom of heaven: his corrupt nature must be removed, and the divine nature come into and control his life. This can be done only by his going to the cross with Me, by faith, and crucifying the old carnal, sinful self. Thus the great plan of salvation is accomplished: the sinful nature is crucified, and through union with Me, he is enabled to live the new life of victory and righteousness."

Notice the Scripture statements about this experience:

"And they that are Christ's have crucified the flesh with the affections and lusts." (Galatians 5:24)

"Now those who belong to Jesus Christ have crucified their lower nature with its passions and appetites." **(Weymouth's Translation)**

This makes it plain that every soul who really becomes a disciple of Christ must experience a crucifixion. *Crucify* means "to put to a violent and painful death." I wonder how many professed Christians, who consider themselves true children of God, have really put the "flesh" to a "violent and painful death." If they have not, how can they be Christ's?

What Is Salvation From Sin?

Jesus saves His people from their sins, but this can be done only by removing the thing which causes us to sin, that is, our fallen nature. No one who is controlled by a fallen, corrupt, selfish nature can stop sinning. God has made no provision to change or reform that nature. It must go to the cross and die, and then God implants within His own divine nature. Many seek to obtain victory by "trying," but God's method is by "dying."

The experience of justification and victory over sin is set forth more fully in Romans 6, 7, and 8 than in any other place in the Bible. The words *death, dead,* and *die* occur 34 times in those three chapters. Every sin we ever commit originates in our sinful nature; therefore if we are ever to stop sinning, that nature must be crucified. We enter into spiritual life through the death of our carnal nature. When by faith we kneel at the foot of the cross and earnestly pray the Lord to take our sinful self up there to share in His death to sin, He answers our prayer. Then His promise is,

"Sin shall not have dominion over you." (Romans 6:14)

"What shall we say then? Shall we continue in sin, that grace may abound? God forbid. How shall we, that are dead to sin, live any longer therein?"   (Romans 6:1, 2)

This spiritual death to sin on the part of God's children is plainly taught in His Word:

"That we, being dead to sins, should live unto righteousness."   (1 Peter 2:24)

"For ye are dead, and your life is hid with Christ in God."   (Colossians 3:3)

"For if we be dead with him, we shall also live with him."   (2 Timothy 2:11)

"Always bearing about in the body the dying of the Lord Jesus."   (2 Corinthians 4:10)

Many sincere Christians are distressed because of besetting sins in their lives, and they long to have victory. Some are troubled with impatience or a bad temper; others may be sensitive and easily offended; some are naturally proud and worldly; others are light and

62

frivolous. All these are manifestations of the fallen nature, and victory and deliverance can be obtained only by dealing with the nature. God has provided no other way, but He makes this way plain:

> **"Know ye not, that so many of us as were baptized into Jesus Christ were baptized into his death? Therefore we are buried with him by baptism into death."**
> **(Romans 6:3, 4)**

Few people seem to understand the real significance of baptism. Scripture baptism, or immersion, symbolizes the burial of one who is dead. It also represents his resurrection. The old nature is crucified by faith. This ceremony of literal burial in the watery grave helps us to realize that the flesh, self, the old man, has been renounced and crucified, and we share with Christ in consigning it to the grave.

> **"Therefore we are buried with him by baptism into death; that like as Christ was raised up from the dead by the glory of the Father, even so we also should walk in newness of life."**
> **(Romans 6:4)**

How unfortunate it is for one to go through the ceremony of immersion without having experienced this death of the old nature and becoming a partaker of the divine nature; for it is this transformation of nature which changes the whole course of life. It delivers us from the bondage of sin and produces in us the life and character of our Saviour. Notice the significance of these words:

> **"We are buried with him by baptism into death."**
> **(Romans 6:4)**

> **"Buried with him in baptism, wherein also ye are risen with him through the faith of the operation of God, who hath raised him from the dead." (Colossians 2:12)**

Lambs Among Wolves

We should earnestly pray that God may guide us in entering fully with Jesus into that experience of death, burial, and resurrection, which will enable us to share His life day by day.

"For if we have been planted together in the likeness of his death, we shall be also in the likeness of his resurrection: knowing this, that our old man is crucified with him, that the body of sin might be destroyed, that henceforth we should not serve sin....Now if we be dead with Christ, we believe that we shall also live with him." **(Romans 6:5–8)**

Often those who seem sincere and long to be free from sin exclaim, "Oh, it is so hard to be good, to overcome my faults, and be a real Christian." Is it not quite evident that they have not understood or applied God's plan?

This experience of crucifying the flesh, or self, of which the Apostle Paul writes fully, was real to him. He declares,

"I am crucified with Christ: nevertheless I live; yet not I, but Christ liveth in me." **(Galatians 2:20)**

In harmony with the teaching of Jesus, Paul tells us that this is a daily experience.

"I protest by your rejoicing which I have in Christ Jesus our Lord, *I die daily*." **(1 Corinthians 15:31)**

It might be well to return a moment to his former statement: "Know ye not that so many of us as were baptized into Jesus Christ were baptized into his death?" (Romans 6:3) It makes a vital difference whether one is baptized into the death of Christ or merely in the water. Did you experience death with Him by faith before you were baptized, or was your baptism simply a ceremony by which you expressed your desire to be a Christian and unite with the church? Was it a testimony to your belief in certain facts or truths, or was it a symbol of an actual spiritual experience? This spiritual death to sin is an experience just as real as physical death. It is by this actual death to sin, by faith, that we enter into the real life in Christ.

He Died to Sin; So Must We

"For in that he died, he died unto sin once: but in that he liveth, he liveth unto God." (Romans 6:10)

It may be helpful here to call attention to the fact that the Bible makes a clear distinction between *sin* and *sins*. Sins are acts of disobedience or transgressions of God's law. (1 John 3:4)

When we think of salvation, it is customary to think of seeking forgiveness, pardon, and cleansing from our sins. We may not stop to think that after we have truly repented and prayed for pardon and claimed God's promises, we go about our work and soon commit the same sin again. Why is this? Let us illustrate sin by a tree, and sins by the fruit on the tree. If the fruit is bad and worthless, we decide to shake it all off and be rid of it. But next year another crop of the same bad, worthless fruit appears.

This illustrates the fact that it is not enough to deal with *sins*. We may commit several sins during the day, and at night repent and confess them, and God forgives us. But the next day we repeat the experience. Is it not evident that salvation must mean more than pardon and cleansing, or we shall go on sinning forever? Pardon deals only with the fruit, but something must be done with the tree which produces the fruit. That tree illustrates what we have called the wolf nature, the flesh, or self.

Jesus died for our sins; and since He bore the penalty for all our transgressions, when we repent and confess them, God forgives, and the record of disobedience is cancelled.

But that does not deal with *sin*, the thing which caused us to transgress. Sins can be pardoned, but *sin* cannot be pardoned, for it is that spirit of rebellion against God, that fallen, selfish, unholy nature, that cannot be changed. Therefore God's only method of dealing with *sin* is *death*.

Jesus in His humanity died unto sin once. When by faith we enter into His death and appropriate it to sin, we are born again and receive the divine nature. (2 Peter 1:4) Then we really belong to the family of God.

"Likewise reckon ye also yourselves to be dead indeed unto *sin*, but alive unto God through Jesus Christ our Lord." **(Romans 6:11)**

I heard of a young man who occupied a position which brought him into contact frequently with a class of dissolute people. There were elements in his nature that responded to the practices of his associates and subjected him to fierce temptations. He professed to be a Christian and resisted the temptations with all his might, but was often near the breaking point. Then he learned the teaching of the Bible regarding this doctrine of death to self, the old carnal nature, which is death to *sin*. By the grace of God he laid hold of the experience. When it seemed necessary to meet those conditions again, he claimed the promises of God, and though brought under fierce temptations, he found to his great joy that a wonderful change had taken place within him. With a deep sense of awe and gratitude he told a friend, "I just seemed to be dead on that side of my nature." That is what God promises to do for those who will follow His plan.

We are not promised freedom from temptation, for the enemy will marshal all his forces against the soul who is determined to "take up his cross" and follow Christ. May God help us to learn to glory in the cross, where our old self is crucified with Christ and we are delivered from the dominion of *sin*. Then we can share in the triumphant cry of the Apostle Paul:

> **"But as for me, God forbid that I should glory in anything except the Cross of our Lord Jesus Christ, upon which the world is crucified to me, and I am crucified to the world."**
>
> **(Galatians 6:14, Weymouth's Translation)**

Lambs Among Wolves

Chapter 6

What Would Jesus Do in My Place?

ONE OF the questions which often perplex those who desire to be real Christians is, How may I know that I am where the Lord wants me to be, and that I am doing what He wants me to do?

Several ways are open before me, but how am I to know which one is His will for me? That this is a problem in which many are interested was demonstrated some decades ago when the book *In His Steps* was written on the subject, and millions of copies were sold.

I read the book at the youthful age when I was not satisfied with beautiful theories. I wanted factual proof, and I questioned any man's ability to tell just what Jesus would do in a world vastly different from that in which He lived 2000 years ago.

When I heard men and women testify that they had resolved to do only what Jesus would do were He in their place, I was rather skeptical. Of course it was a fine motto and a commendable ideal, if it were only possible to know what He would do. I reasoned it all out for myself. I said, "Suppose here is a boy whose parents were millionaires, but they were killed in an accident. The boy is left with a palatial home and millions of dollars. His circumstances are entirely different from those of Jesus when He was that age. How could he possibly know what Jesus would do in his place?" I thought of many such illustrations. I decided that all this discussion of what Jesus would do was mere speculation and was based entirely on the imagination of the author.

But as I studied God's Word more carefully, I learned that when any soul for whom He had laid down His life has a deep longing to know God's plan for him, and will study God's Word, and pray, the Lord will demonstrate His love by making the way perfectly plain. I believe we shall be able to show definitely from the Bible that every child of His may know day by day—in every plan, activity, and decision—just what Jesus would do in his place. This may seem surprising, but is it not reasonable to think that One who has infinite wisdom, and loves us with infinite love, is able and willing to guide us day by day in this dark world?

Natural and Spiritual Laws

In the physical world we recognize that everything is governed by what we term the laws of nature. There are natural laws which must be observed in relation to all animal life and all plant life. Also all the inanimate forces of nature are subject to laws, and the better we understand these laws, the more benefit we derive from these forces. We have learned something of the laws that prevail in the realm of electricity, and by working in harmony with those laws, we can obtain light, heat, and power. But to ignore or defy the laws of electricity will rob us of its benefits and may bring instant death.

The vast advance in industry during the past century, and also in mechanics and scientific inventions for the benefit of mankind, is the result of study and research and new discoveries in this realm of natural law.

This suggests a logical question. Is it possible that the Creator of this vast universe has placed all things, animate and inanimate, subject to natural law, while in the higher sphere of spiritual life He has left everything in uncertainty, subject to mere chance? We know this could not be. Therefore we must conclude that when we come into full harmony with the spiritual laws ordained by our Creator, we may achieve any end and reach any ideal or goal He has placed before us.

The First Step in God's Plan

There are many beautiful lessons and illustrations in the Bible which seem plain and simple, yet we do not get their deep significance unless we study them and meditate upon them. Looking out into the yard, I see a large grapevine. It has scores of branches and hundreds of leaves, yet we look upon it as just one vine. Jesus used it to illustrate a fundamental truth: "I am the vine, ye are the branches." (John 15:5) The branches are not separate from the vine—they are all one. So Jesus uses the vine to show the relation of Christians to Christ and to one another. When we are born again, we are brought into such a union with Him that we are said to be members of His body:

"Now ye are the body of Christ, and members in particular." **(1 Corinthians 12:27)**

It is of the greatest importance for us to cultivate constantly the consciousness of this union with Him if we are to know His will for us.

"And he that keepeth his commandments dwelleth in him, and he in him." **(1 John 3:24)**

"He that dwelleth in love dwelleth in God, and God in him." **(1 John 4:16)**

"Abide in me, and I in you. As the branch cannot bear fruit of itself, except it abide in the vine; no more can ye, except ye abide in me....He that abideth in me, and I

in him, the same bringeth forth much fruit: for without me ye can do nothing."   (John 15:4, 5)

"Behold, I stand at the door and knock: if any man hear my voice, and open the door, I will come in to him, and will sup with him, and he with me."
(Revelation 3:20)

It is this union with Christ by faith which brings us into harmony with His laws. So we read,

"Herein is our love made perfect, that we may have boldness in the day of judgment, because as he is, so are we in this world."   (1 John 4:17)

We have looked forward to our home in heaven, believing that when we are translated to that glorious land, we shall be like Him. But this verse says, "As he is, so are we *in this world*." If we are living in union with Him as the branch is united to the vine, His life flows continuously into our lives. Therefore "as he is so are we."

"Every child lives by the life of his father. If you are God's children,—begotten by His Spirit,—you live by the life of God. In Christ dwells 'all the fullness of the Godhead bodily;' and the life of Jesus is made manifest 'in our mortal flesh.' That life in you will produce the same character and manifest the same works as it did in Him."[1]

The Next Step

We have found that God's ideal may be reached only as we live in harmony with spiritual law; we believe Jesus set the example by living in perfect harmony with that law. When we study His life and the law by which He overcame all the snares and temptations of Satan, we

---

1   Ellen G. White, *Thoughts From the Mount of Blessing* (Mountain View: Pacific Press Publishing Association, 1955) 118.

have found the key which will make that life available to us. Here is that wonderful key:

"I can of mine own self do nothing."　　(John 5:30)

This is the first step. If you would know what Christ would do if He were in your place, it is absolutely necessary to start here, where He started. Many have mistaken ideas of Christ's life in humanity. They say that Christ was divine, He was God, and He could do anything, and so they brush His statement aside. But Jesus makes His position plain when He says,

"I can of mine own self do nothing:...because I seek not mine own will, but the will of the Father which hath sent me."　　(John 5:30)

Two Wills

This statement brings before us the fact that there are two wills: "mine own will" and "the will of the Father which sent me." Sin and righteousness are matters of the will. There is a right way to exercise the will, and there is a wrong way. Sin entered the universe as a result of the wrong use of the will. When a created being exercises his will contrary to the will of his Creator, he is in rebellion against the government of the universe. That is what cast Lucifer out of heaven.

"How art thou fallen from heaven, O Lucifer, son of the morning! How art thou cut down to the ground, which didst weaken the nations! For thou hast said in thine heart, I will ascend into heaven, I will exalt my throne above the stars of God: I will sit also upon the mount of the congregation, in the sides of the north: I will ascend above the heights of the clouds; I will be like the most High."　　(Isaiah 14:12–14)

Lucifer refused to recognize any authority above himself. That principle transformed him from a glorious

73

angel into a devil. Following that principle will produce the same result in any created being. Thus we understand that "everything depends upon the right action of the will."

Let us notice the contrast between Lucifer and Christ, in the way each one exercised his will. When Jesus finished His public ministry and entered upon the experience of taking the sinner's condemnation and penalty, He experienced agony of soul beyond anything which we can comprehend. The Bible tells us:

"And he went a little farther, and fell on his face, and prayed, saying, O my Father, if it be possible, let this cup pass from me: nevertheless not as I will, but as thou wilt." **(Matthew 26:39)**

Here, in the supreme test of His life, He demonstrated that He came not to do His own will but the will of His Father. The only obstruction to the complete working out of God's plan in the life of any individual is the will. God could carry out His purpose in every human being if the will were fully yielded to Him.

God made man a free moral agent, with ability to obey the law of the government of heaven and to develop a character that would entitle him to live forever. But he listened to the alluring lies of the fallen Lucifer and decided to obey him instead of God. Thus the human will was weakened, perverted, and made incapable of maintaining God's pure and holy standard. God might have destroyed Adam and Eve because of their disobedience, but He is LOVE, and in His infinite mercy He revealed His plan to give man another chance.

The Way Back

Jesus came to this fallen world and became a member of the human family; that is why He usually spoke of Himself as the Son of man.

"Forasmuch then as the children are partakers of flesh and blood, he also himself likewise took part of the same; . . . for verily he took not on him the nature of angels; but he took on him the seed of Abraham."
(Hebrews 2:14–16)

"But when the fulness of the time was come, God sent forth his Son, made of a woman, made under the law."
(Galatians 4:4)

Jesus was filled with the Holy Spirit. He was, therefore, enabled to keep His will surrendered to the Father, thus removing every hindrance to the perfect working out of God's will in Him. The life of Jesus on earth is God's ideal for every human being. It reveals just how God would work out His plan in each individual if the will were fully yielded to Him.

We cannot be saved. unless we are born again. (John 3:3) And when we are born again, we receive the gift of the Holy Spirit, who comes to dwell in us and make our bodies His temple. (Acts 2:38; 1 Corinthians 6:19) We may have the same power dwelling in us to enable us to keep the will surrendered to the Father, as Jesus did. And thus the Father will produce in us the same character as He did in Jesus.

When we read the story of the storm upon the lake (Mark 4), which threatened to sink the disciples' boat, we are not surprised that Jesus "rebuked the wind, and said unto the sea, Peace, be still....And there was a great calm." It seems easy to say He could do that, for He was "the Master of earth, and sea, and sky"; He was the Son of God. It also seems easy to forget His own words, "I can of

75

mine own self do nothing." Jesus was not exercising divine power in His own behalf, but He had come as the Son of man to demonstrate how we can live by bringing our lives into harmony with the spiritual law which governed His life.

"When Jesus was awakened to meet the storm, He was in perfect peace. There was no trace of fear in word or look, for no fear was in His heart. But He rested not in possession of almighty power. It was not as the 'Master of earth and sea and sky' that He reposed in quiet. That power He had laid down, and He says, 'I can of Mine own self do nothing.' He trusted in the Father's might. It was in faith—faith in God's love and care—that Jesus rested, and the power of that word which stilled the storm was the power of God."[1]

Jesus makes it plain that if the disciples had possessed the faith offered them, they could have stilled the storm as readily as He did.

"And he arose, and rebuked the wind, and said unto the sea, Peace, be still. And the wind ceased, and there was a great calm. And he said unto them, why are ye so fearful? How is it that ye have no faith?"

(Mark 4:39, 40)

These lessons reveal the fact that if we relate ourselves to the laws of spiritual life as Jesus did, there will be no failure in our Christian experience. Should we not cultivate in our minds and hearts the thought, "Heavenly Father, I am not here to do my own will, but Thy will"? This will enable Him to live out His life in us.

---

1   Ellen G. White, *The Desire of Ages*, 336.

God Was in Christ

When Jesus was here on earth He was tried and tempted, but He was ever conscious that the Father was dwelling within Him and working through Him.

"Wherefore in all things it behoved him to be made like unto his brethren....For in that he himself hath suffered being tempted, he is able to succour them that are tempted."   **(Hebrews 2:17, 18)**

"Then Jesus said unto them, When ye have lifted up the Son of man, then shall ye know that I am he, and that I do nothing of myself; but as my Father hath taught me, I speak these things."   **(John 8:28)**

Jesus maintained that consciousness of the presence of God with Him continuously, yielding His will so fully that all He said and all He did came from the Father. This is what Jesus would do today if He were in your place. It is what He desires you to do. If we look at those about us, pointing out their faults, criticizing their conduct, and perhaps quarreling with them, we are following the law of death rather than of life. By "beholding others" and losing sight of Him, we get into darkness and failure and sin. But by beholding Him we are "changed into the same image from glory to glory."

Here is the statement of the Apostle Paul, summing up the whole gospel:

"Christ in you, the hope of glory." As God was in Christ, so Christ is to be in each one of His followers. "Know ye not your own selves, how that Jesus Christ is in you, except ye be reprobates?" (2 Corinthians 13:5)

Two Wills in One

We have considered Christ's words, "I Came...not to do mine own will, but the will of him that sent me." We might conclude from this statement that there were two conflicting wills, and that it was a constant struggle for Christ to keep His will subject to that of His Father. But we need to place with this another striking statement of the Saviour:

"I and my Father are one." John 10:30.

Here is a further revelation of the wonderful law of the spiritual life. When Jesus accepted the Father's will as His own, their wills merged, so there was never any conflict.

Who could conceive of a more wonderful experience than to have Jesus abiding in us and our wills so fully surrendered to Him that they are merged with His will, and we can say, "Jesus and I are one"? This is His plan.

"When we submit ourselves to Christ, the heart is united with His heart, the will is merged in His will, the mind becomes one with His mind, the thoughts are brought into captivity to Him; we live His life. This is what it means to be clothed with the garment of His righteousness.

"And if we consent, He will so identify Himself with our thoughts and aims, so blend our hearts and minds into conformity with His will, that when obeying Him we shall be but carrying out our own impulses. The will, refined and sanctified, will find its highest delight in doing His service. When we know God as it is our privilege to know Him, our life will be a life of continual obedience. Through an appreciation of the character of Christ, through communion with God, sin will become hateful to us."[1]

"God was in Christ," and their wills were so merged that Jesus did only what the Father desired Him to do and spoke what the Father would have Him speak. His life was in every respect a revelation of the Father.

---

1   Ellen G. White, *The Desire of Ages*, 668.

"Philip saith unto him, Lord, shew us the Father, and it sufficeth us. Jesus saith unto him, Have I been so long time with you, and yet hast thou not known me, Philip? he that hath seen me hath seen the Father; and how sayest thou then, Shew us the Father?"

(John 14:8, 9)

There was a note of disappointment in the words of Jesus, as though He would say, "What you have seen as you have been with Me all these months has been the Father. I and My Father are one. As He is, so am I in the world. As you have seen the sick healed, the blind eyes opened, the lame walk, and the lepers cleansed, you have seen the Father working. As you have heard the words of love and mercy, the calls to repentance and salvation, you have heard the Father speaking."

His Glorious Plan for Us

We have had plainly set forth from the Bible the relation of Christ to the Father when He was here on earth. Now if it can be shown from the same Word that our relation to Christ is to be identical with His relation to the Father, we would clearly understand the meaning of His statement, "As he is, so are we in this world." In His prayer to the Father, Jesus revealed this:

"As thou hast sent me into the world, even so have I also sent them into the world....And the glory which thou gavest me I have given them; that they may be one, even as we are one; I in them, and thou in me, that they may be made perfect in one; and that the world may know that thou hast sent me, and hast loved them, as thou hast loved me."   **(John 17:18, 22, 23)**

We co-operate and work in harmony with the natural laws of the physical world in order to obtain the benefits provided for us by our Creator. Is it not perfectly evident that in God's plan of love for us He expects us to conform to the law of spiritual life, to bring our wills into harmony with His will? Thus we may know each day and each hour that we are abiding in God's will. We may have the peace and joy of the consciousness that we are where our Father wants us and are carrying out His purpose for us. We may have the experience of the Apostle Paul:

"I am crucified with Christ: nevertheless I live; yet not I, but Christ liveth in me." **(Galatians 2:20)**

Chapter 7

Don't Be a Fool

WE CANNOT say that one of Christ's parables is more important than another, for everyone contains lessons which He knew would be needed by His disciples. But we know that the enemy of our souls will do all in his power to lead us to neglect the lesson which would bring us the greatest help. The Lord gave a parable about a rich man, and many of us might say that since we are not in his class, we need not give special study to that parable. However, if we give this lesson careful thought, we shall see how important it is for every individual.

"And he spake a parable unto them, saying, The ground of a certain rich man brought forth plentifully: and he thought within himself, saying, What shall I do, because I have no room where to bestow my fruits? And he said, This will I do: I will pull down my barns, and build greater; and there will I bestow all my fruits and my goods. And I will say to my soul, Soul, thou hast much goods laid up for many years; take thine ease, eat, drink, and be merry. But God said unto him, Thou fool, this night thy soul shall be required of thee: then whose shall those things be which thou hast provided? So is he that layeth up treasure for himself, and is not rich toward God." (Luke 12:16–21)

Because of His great love and mercy God is frank in speaking to sinful men. Nothing can be concealed from Him. He tells us just what we are so that we may turn from our sins and be saved. We can imagine that the people in the community where this rich man lived esteemed him highly. He may have been educated, cultured, a social and political leader. But however highly he might have been regarded by men, God called him a fool.

We can hardly think of anything that arouses our resentment more than being called a fool, and we avoid any course that would provoke people to call us by that name. Are we as careful to avoid having God regard us as fools?

Let us seek to understand just why God called this man a fool. We cannot believe it was because his ground "brought forth plentifully," for that is often true of the ground of poor men, and we know it is the blessing of God that causes crops to flourish.

The man lacked room to store his crops, so he proposed to build larger barns. Since it was by the blessing of God that he obtained the large harvest, surely the Lord would not condemn him for taking care of all of it.

After this provision was made, he said to his soul, "Soul, thou hast much goods laid up for many years." Just how many years did this man know that he would live to enjoy these fruits? He did not know. He may have been well and strong, in the prime of life, and assumed that he had many years to live. He was very much interested in his soul's enjoyment of the things of this life, but did he have no regard for his soul's eternal welfare? Perhaps he did. I meet few people who say they have no interest in the future life. But he was sure there was plenty of time; why not enjoy life now and prepare for eternity later? He was prosperous. He had reached the goal which appeals so strongly to the world today, which is commonly called "security." But is security for this life more important than security for eternity?

And so, alas, he complacently went to sleep, unprepared to meet God, and he never wakened! That is why God called him a fool. What could any intelligent being in this world do that would constitute him so great a fool as to go to bed and to sleep, unprepared to meet God, while knowing that he might never waken? As I have traveled over the world, my heart has been stirred with sorrow and pity to see how lightly the great masses of people seem to regard eternity. Eternity is a long, long time. How foolish it is to go complacently about our work or play, giving little or no thought to eternal things, and then going to bed at night unprepared to meet God!

Speaking to a large congregation, I said to a fine-looking youth sitting before me, "If I should bring you a legal document declaring that for the sum of $1000 you would give up all hope of eternal life, would you sign the paper if I gave you the money?" He replied, "No, sir, I would not."

"Well," I said, "suppose we make it $100,000; would you sign the paper for that much?"

Again he said, "No, sir."

"Suppose we make it $1,000,000; would you sign it then?"

"No, sir."

"All right," I said, "let us make it $10,000,000."

Without hesitation he said, "No, sir."

Perhaps the majority of people would reply as that youth did, yet I fear that millions are throwing away *eternity* for a dollar or less. How many there are who know that they commit sins during the day, but who retire at night, unprepared to meet God!

In these prosperous days it may be well to note that the rich man's problem was what to do with his large crops, which were more than his barns would hold. No doubt there were needy people about him, but he thought only of himself. God had blessed him that he might be a blessing to those who were in want, and thus bring spiritual blessing to his own life. But he held on to his riches, thinking only of his own enjoyment. Instead of expressing his love to God and his gratitude for the Lord's wonderful blessings, his appreciation for all these things was manifested in the words to his soul, "Take thine ease, eat, drink, and be merry."

Dangers We All Face

There are many reasons why we should be prepared to meet God at any time. One is presented in the last chapter of the Bible:

"And he saith unto me, Seal not the sayings of the prophecy of this book: for the time is at hand. He that is unjust, let him be unjust still: and he which is filthy, let him be filthy still: and he that is righteous, let him be righteous still: and he that is holy, let him be holy still. And, behold, I come quickly; and my reward is with me, to give every man according as his work shall be." (Revelation 22:10–12)

We know from the words of Christ in Matthew 24 and from many other prophecies of the Bible that the time of the coming of Christ in glory and the end of this world is drawing near. We also know that before He leaves the sanctuary in heaven, where He has been ministering in behalf of sinners, He will finish the judgment work and make the solemn announcement just quoted, which marks the close of human probation. After that announcement is made, there will be no more salvation for sinners, for he that is holy, will be holy still, and he that is filthy, will be filthy still.

Don't Be a Fool

"What we make of ourselves in probationary time, that we must remain to all eternity."[1]

We may ask, When will probation close? That question no human being can answer. But we do know that the Saviour said:

"And take heed to yourselves, lest at any time your hearts be overcharged with surfeiting, and drunkenness, and cares of this life, and so that day come upon you unawares. For as a snare shall it come on all them that dwell on the face of the whole earth."
(Luke 21:34, 35)

What unspeakable folly to be so occupied with the cares, riches, and pleasures of this life that we shall be unprepared when probation closes, and thus lose all eternity in that better world!

I have heard many say, "Well, I do not do anything very bad, and I am trying to do right. I think that if I do the best I can, when probation closes, the Lord will take care of me." Would it not be more sensible to believe that God means what He says, that when probation closes and we are filthy, we shall be filthy still; but if we are holy, we shall be holy still? God has placed the standard before us, and through a life of surrender and obedience we can reach the goal.

Another reason why we should be prepared to meet God at any time is the uncertainty of life. Not a soul upon earth knows of a certainty that he will be alive tomorrow; therefore the time to prepare for eternity is *today*. Some are putting it off, thinking that when trouble and adversity come, they will seek the Lord. They are taking a terrible chance.

One evening some years ago I went with a group of fine young people to a place a few miles out in the country for a

---

1   Ellen G. White, *Testimonies for the Church*, vol. 5, 466.

85

picnic. The boys gathered some wood and started a fire, for it was rather cool. Then someone suggested exercising before eating the lunch. They gathered in a large circle and played a game in which two persons would chase another around the circle. As I stood watching them, a young girl and a middle-aged lady started to run. After a few steps the lady stopped, laid off her heavy coat, and then started to run again. After a few steps more, she hesitated and quietly sank to the ground. We gathered around her, but she was unconscious. As we did not know what the trouble was, we placed her in the auto, and our leader took her back to the city.

We sat around the campfire and ate our lunch, and I told the young people stories of the mission fields. At nine o'clock the pastor returned and told us that the woman was dead when we placed her in the car. It deeply impressed me with the uncertainty of life. I realized that when she sank down upon the sand, her eternal destiny was fixed, for "what we make of ourselves in probationary time, that we must remain to all eternity." There will be no change in anyone's character while he is in the grave, and there will be no change in the character when Jesus comes.

He will "change our vile body, that it may be fashioned like unto his glorious body"; "this mortal shall have put on immortality," but our characters will not be changed.

All through the centuries pagan philosophers have argued, "Let us eat, drink, and be merry, for tomorrow we die." They saw little or no hope for life beyond the grave; so they said, "Let us enjoy ourselves, and have a good time, for tomorrow we die." They had no goal for the future, no prospect beyond this life.

But the Christian philosophy is altogether different; it always has been. The Christian says, "I am living in this world under the awful tragedy of sin and rebellion against God. But through His love and mercy I am granted this brief life of probation, with the privilege of developing a character, by His divine grace, which will entitle me to spend eternity in a glorious new world which will be purified from the last vestige of sin. My goal is over there. When trials, afflictions, and disappointments come, I can take it patiently and cheerfully, for my loving heavenly Father knows what it will take to develop the character all must have over there."

Another Peril of the Last Days

One of the greatest dangers for God's people today is the tidal wave of paganism that has swept over the world the past 80 years, by which many who really desire to be saved may be unconsciously influenced. The enemy suggests to young people, "Let's have a good time today; we are only young once, and there is nothing essentially wrong in this amusement or pleasure." The dreadful experience of the demoniac of Capernaum, as recorded in Mark 1:23–26, may well be considered by the youth of today. Mrs. E. G. White has this comment to make:

"The secret cause of the affliction that had made man a fearful spectacle to his friends and a burden to himself was in his own life. He had been fascinated by the pleasures of sin, and had thought to make his life a grand carnival. He did not dream of becoming a terror to the world and the reproach of his family. He thought his time could be spent in innocent folly. But once on the downward path, his feet rapidly descended. Intemperance and frivolity perverted the noble attributes of his nature, and Satan took absolute control of him.

"Remorse came too late. When he would have sacrificed wealth and pleasure to regain his lost manhood, he had become helpless in the grasp of the evil one. He had placed himself on the enemy's ground, and Satan had taken possession of all his faculties. The tempter had allured him with many charming presentations;

but when once the wretched man was in his power, the fiend became relentless in his cruelty, and terrible in his angry visitations. So it will be with all who yield to evil; the fascinating pleasure of their early career ends in the darkness of despair or the madness of a ruined soul."[1]

In view of the fact that probation will close in heaven before long, and also because life in this world is uncertain and may end suddenly and unexpectedly, is it not sensible and actually imperative that we consider just what we should do day by day so as to be prepared at any time to meet God and make sure of eternity in His kingdom? What is more important, more imperative?

If This Were My Last Day

There is only one way by which we can escape the danger of the foolish rich man, and that is to be prepared to meet God at any time. If I should live today just as God wants me to live and should die tonight, I am sure of eternal life. But if I should not die, and should live the same tomorrow and every day, and my life is extended for months or years, I have nothing to regret, for the greatest satisfaction in this world comes from living in harmony with the will of God. Let me suggest seven things which I believe every intelligent Christian would do if he knew this were his last day in this world.

ONE

If I knew this were my last day, I would not go to sleep tonight until I had made everything right with God. We understand from the Bible that a record of our lives is kept in heaven. All our words, our deeds, and our thoughts are recorded there; and in the judgment that

---

1   Ellen G. White, *The Desire of Ages*, 256.

record will be the basis upon which our eternal reward or punishment will be decided. When I come to God and humbly and sincerely confess a sin, asking His pardon in the name of Jesus, He forgives me, and that sin is canceled. If I thus repent and confess every sin, I know that if I die tonight, as far as the record is concerned, all is well. But if there are sins unrepented, unconfessed, I have lost all eternity.

TWO

The second thing I would do if I knew this were my last day would be to make everything right with my fellow men. If we have wronged God, we must make that right; but it is just as necessary to make right the wrongs we have done to other human beings. "The wages of sin is death," and the only way we can escape the wages is to repent and confess the sin and by faith claim pardon through the merits of Jesus our Redeemer.

A young lady attending an academy told me her experience. She was regarded as a fine Christian girl. After hearing my sermon on making things right, she went home thinking seriously of its application in her own life. She was afraid to go to bed, for she remembered having cheated in an examination some weeks before. She dreaded to confess such a thing to her teacher, who esteemed her highly, but finally decided there was no other way. She found the teacher and in deep contrition confessed her wrong. The teacher was kind and forgave her, and they prayed together. She went back to her room, but was still afraid to retire. She finally went to the lady in whose house she worked, and confessed that occasionally while working about the house alone, she had taken fruit or nuts from the table, though she realized they did not belong to her. The lady freely forgave her.

The girl then went to her room, and as she bowed in earnest prayer, she was profoundly impressed with the consciousness that Jesus was in the room with her. She told me she never knew such an experience was possible, and she was determined day by day to keep everything right between her and God, and between her and her fellow man.

Many times youth have told me of having yielded to temptation to steal, perhaps something of no great value, or to tell a falsehood, or commit some other act which they knew to be wrong. Happily many of them have made those things right and have gained peace of mind.

THREE

If I knew this were my last day, I would take some time to study God's Word. We all claim that we believe the Bible, though many have not read it through. How can we be sure we believe a Book we have never read? We are told that the Word of God is to the spiritual life what food is to the physical life. If we would not think of starving our physical bodies, but neglect to take spiritual food, is that not evidence that we place a higher value on mere physical existence? We need to realize that it is not enough just to read a little here and there in the Bible or even to read the Bible through; we must study it until our hearts are stirred with a consciousness that it is a personal message from our heavenly Father.

By way of illustration is the following experience, which has been an inspiration to me for many years. A young lady sent word that she would like to have me bring another minister to her home and have prayer for her healing. We found her to be a young woman eighteen years of age, who had undergone eight major surgical operations. Some of the most skillful surgeons in the land had done their best, yet she was still far from well. We were told that when one of them was asked what he thought of the prospect for her recovery, he said, "She will die unless she has another operation, and she will die if she has another operation."

We prayed for her, and God healed her. The next year I visited her occasionally at the college she was attending. I always enjoyed talking with her, for I had never seen anyone to whom Jesus seemed more real than to her. One day she was telling me about how definitely and lovingly God had spoken to her through His Word.

"I was in the hospital awaiting my seventh major operation," she said. "I was so nervous and so full of pain from head to foot that it seemed as though I could not go through the ordeal again. I picked up this little Bible and said, 'Dear Jesus, will You please say something that will help me through this operation today?' I let the Bible fall open, and my eyes fell upon these words:

"'Behold, happy is the man whom God correcteth: therefore despise not thou the chastening of the Almighty: for he maketh sore, and bindeth up: he woundeth, and his hands make whole. He shall deliver thee in six troubles: yea, in seven there shall no evil touch thee.' (Job 5:17–19)**

"I said, 'Thank You, Jesus; I know that will take me through,' and it did."

For nearly 40 years since then she has been serving Him earnestly and devotedly. Truly we never face a trial, or a problem, or a crisis in our lives that God has not made provision for. The help we need may be found in His Word. Since I know that this may be my last day, I believe it is wise to search His Word, humbly asking Him to give me the message I need.

FOUR

If I knew this were my last day, I would take time to pray. In order to impress one point in this matter of prayer upon the minds of the people, I have sometimes asked a congregation, "How many of you say your prayers every night before you go to bed?" Usually the large majority raise their hands, and they look at me with amazement when I advise them not to do it again. Of course they expect an explanation.

I believe there is a great difference between "saying your prayers" and praying. As a child my mother taught me a little prayer, and I said it quite faithfully every night, though I know that when tired or sleepy, I gave it little thought. But as I now think back upon my youthful days, I realize that it is an easy matter to "say" a prayer while thinking of something else.

Some years ago I was a member of a party traveling to Tibet. We had left Chungking in western China and had traversed mountain trails for hundreds of miles through bandit-infested country. Often the scenery was beautiful, and the bandits added to the interest by taking an occasional shot at us.

At last we reached the country inhabited by Tibetan tribesmen. I soon noticed strips of paper about two feet long and several inches wide, covered with strange-looking characters, hanging in bunches from the limbs of the trees. I asked a companion what they were for. He explained that the priests wrote prayers on these strips of paper, and the people hung them up where the wind would blow them back and forth. Thus their prayers would be going on all the time while they were busy with other things. Often we would see Tibetan priests approaching, each one carrying in his hand a round wooden box with a handle. They were continually whirling these boxes as they walked along, and they did not stop even while talking with us. I asked the meaning of this performance and was told that the boxes were called prayer wheels and contained prayers which they kept in motion hours at a time. Probably Christians in our land would not do that, yet I think we are inclined to drift more or less into formality unless we are keenly conscious that we are conversing with a real Person.

Many years ago I was "saying my prayers" one night, when it seemed as though a voice whispered to me, "Would you say what you are saying if you should open your eyes and see the Lord standing right before you?" I was rather startled and tried to think just what I had been saying. But I forgot the lesson, and a few nights later I was saying my prayers again. Then that voice again asked, "Would you say what you are saying if you should open your eyes and see the Lord standing there looking at you?" Instantly I thought, "No, I would not." And then the question came, "What would you say?" I concentrated my thought upon that question earnestly for several minutes, conscious that I was facing a real crisis in my prayer life. It was the introduction to one of the most precious and important experiences of my life. I determined to say nothing until I was sure it was just what I would say if I were face to face with Him.

Then, quietly the voice spoke again, "Lo, I am with you always, even unto the end of the world. I will never leave thee, nor forsake thee." I was profoundly moved, for I knew that Jesus was there with me. In deep contrition I talked with Him, and prayer was a new experience to me.

FIVE

The fifth thing I would do if I knew this were my last day would be to cultivate a love for heavenly things. Colossians 3:1, 2 reads, "If ye then be risen with Christ, seek those things which are above, where Christ sitteth on the right hand of God. Set your affection on things above, not on things on the earth."

I believe that if we cultivate a love for heavenly things day by day, we shall feel right at home when we reach heaven. But one who is absorbed in shows, dances, hilarious parties, commercialized sports and games, and the amusement of self is certainly not prepared to enjoy and appreciate the pleasures of heaven. There is a principle involved here which many do not seem to understand. They want to be saved, so they try to overcome the desire to do the things they want to do but are told are wrong. Their whole attitude is reversed when they have learned the true principle stated by a well-known religious teacher:

> **"Temptation has no power over the one whose heart is already thrilled with the love of things divine....Love not the world, neither the things that are in the world. If any man love the world, the love of the Father is not in him. For all that is in the world, the lust of the flesh, and the lust of the eyes, and the pride of life, is not of the Father, but is of the world. And the world passeth away, and the lust thereof: but he that doeth the will of God abideth forever." (1 John 2:15–17)**

SIX

If I knew this were my last day, I would strive to have my conversation pleasing to my Saviour and helpful to others. The Lord gives us definite instruction on this subject:

> **"But I say unto you, That every idle word that men shall speak, they shall give account thereof in the day of judgment. For by thy words thou shalt be justified, and by thy words thou shalt be condemned." (Matthew 12:36, 37)**

It is natural for some of us to indulge in a continuous round of jesting, joking, and foolish talking. Others indulge in gossip, criticism, and slang expressions. All these things go out of our lives when Jesus becomes real to us; and we then seek by kind, courteous, helpful conversation to exert an elevating, ennobling influence over all with whom we associate.

SEVEN

If I knew this were my last day, I would watch for every opportunity to do some definite service for my Master. Let us think again of the man God called a fool. He was absorbed in his own affairs. He had all that he needed for himself, but apparently he had no interest in those about him who were in need, and whom he could have helped—and God called him a fool. Selfishness never produces real happiness. Unselfish love for God and for our fellow men brings a joy and satisfaction we can get in no other way.

When the Lord comes with His rewards, we want Him to say to us, "Well done, thou good and faithful servant." How could He say that to one who has spent his life in serving himself and living to have what the world calls a good time?

Let us make this seven-point program practical by keeping it in our minds and by practicing it every day:

Keep everything right with our God every day.

Keep everything right with our fellow men every day.

Take time daily to study God's Word.

Spend time every day in earnest prayer and contact with the Lord.

Cultivate a love for heavenly things.

Be careful of our conversation.

Improve every opportunity to witness for Jesus in word and deed.

May I ask you a personal question? Have you been living like the foolish man, just thinking about having a good time and enjoying yourself? Have you been doing things you know were not pleasing to God? Have you been careless and neglectful of these essential things? If your life had suddenly been snatched away in an accident, would you have lost all eternity? If so, will you lift your heart in earnest prayer right now: "Oh, God, I am determined by Thy grace to begin this very hour to live for eternity. I cannot, I will not, be a fool and run the risk of losing eternity, the life which Thou hast provided for me at infinite cost."

Chapter 8

The Supreme Goal of Life

SOME PEOPLE seem to have the idea that the chief object of becoming a Christian is to make sure of getting to heaven. That is a rather narrow view. Adam and Eve were created in the image of God. In their physical, mental, and spiritual nature they bore a likeness to their Creator. Through disobedience that likeness was marred and well-nigh obliterated. Logically, then, salvation would be the restoration of the divine image, bringing men back to purity and holiness and communion with their Creator. Here we find the main object of Christianity.

In this process of restoration, however, we cannot be passive, merely submitting to an arbitrary act of God. His plan is that we choose to be restored and co-operate with Him with all our will and energies in developing a Christlike character.

Though we are fallen, sinful creatures, God loves us and has set before us His glorious plan to re-create us in His image and to make us fit to share in the indescribable joy and happiness of eternal life in His kingdom. The Bible says,

"Know ye that the Lord he is God: it is he that hath made us, and not we ourselves; we are his people, and the sheep of his pasture." **(Psalm 100:3)**

When God says, "It is he that hath made us," we may assume that He refers to creation, or we may feel that when we are born again and become His children, He has made us anew. Both views are correct. But it would also be well for us to consider that we are in the process of being made here in this life; consequently, it is of the greatest importance for us to study and understand God's plan so that we can co-operate intelligently with Him.

Let us think just a moment about our first study—how we come into this world with a fallen, sinful, wolf nature. Then, the first thing that Jesus must do in the work of restoration is to take these selfish, sinful wolves and make them lambs. And we know very well that this is not something we can do for ourselves; only God can re-create a wolf and make it a lamb. After performing this wonderful miracle of transformation from a wolf to a lamb, He tells us that we are His people, and the sheep of His pasture.

Then Jesus the great Shepherd says, "Go your ways: behold, I send you forth as lambs among wolves." (Luke 10:3) At first thought this seems shocking. Just imagine looking out into the woods and seeing a pack of ugly, vicious wolves and a little innocent lamb walking into their midst. Your astonishment deepens when you realize that the shepherd who loves the lamb sent it out. Jesus has done this with His lambs, and He has a reason: There are wolves to be won.

Jesus gives His loving invitation, "Follow me," and then He says, "I will make you fishers of men." There is the great goal set before His followers, the supreme goal of the Christian life. It is true that the Bible says,

"Believe on the Lord Jesus Christ, and thou shalt be saved." **(Acts 16:31)**

But could anyone truly believe on the Lord Jesus Christ and not obey Him? Many have been deceived on this

point; they have been told that good works are not necessary in the Christian life. But they forget that the Bible
also says,

"Faith, if it hath not works, is dead."   (James 2:17, 18)

**"For we are his workmanship, created in Christ Jesus
unto good works, which God hath before ordained that
we should walk in them."   (Ephesians 2:10)**

The Bible says we are not saved by good works but for
good works, and without good works there is no evidence
of salvation.

**"For we are God's own handiwork, created in Christ
Jesus for good works which He has pre-destined us to
practise."   (Ephesians 2: 10, Weymouth's Translation)**

This is also made clear in the statement,

*"Man is to be saved by faith, not by works; yet his faith
must be shown by his works."[1]*

Let me illustrate the meaning of the expression "We
are his workmanship." While traveling in many lands,
often among people whose language I could not understand, I experienced real homesickness. Many times I
looked down the street of a large city, saw an automobile
coming, and almost involuntarily said, "Ah, there comes
a Ford!" What a thrill it was, in a faraway land, to see a
Ford. But what did I mean by saying, "There comes a
Ford"? I meant that a man by the name of Ford manufac-
tured autos by the millions, and they may be seen in
almost any country in the world. How did I know that it
was not a Buick, or a Chevrolet, or a Plymouth? It was
because of the workmanship. Mr. Ford had a pattern, and
all his cars were made after that pattern, so they were
easily distinguished from any other cars.

1   Ellen G. White, *Patriarchs and Prophets* (Washington D.C.: Review
and Herald Publishing Association, 1958) 279.

God's Pattern

I believe this illustrates in a way what God means when He says, "We are his workmanship." God is making something far more important than automobiles. He is making characters, citizens for His eternal kingdom. He is taking the poor, miserable, shattered wrecks that sin has made and is transforming them by His grace into new men and women. And God has a pattern; it is found in Romans 8:9: "For whom he did foreknow, he also did predestinate, to be conformed to the image of his Son."

Jesus came to earth and lived such a perfect life that the Father declared, "This is my beloved Son, in whom I am well pleased." It is God's purpose, moreover, that every soul redeemed from this fallen race shall develop a character after the Pattern. He tells us that we are to "put on the new man, which, after God, is created in righteousness and true holiness." (Ephesians 4:24) We are told that

"...those who receive the seal of the living God and are protected in the time of trouble must reflect the image of Jesus fully."[1]

Let us look at the practical side of this question. What does it mean to be a Christian? According to the Word of God, it means that His image is to be restored in us; we are to become like Christ, who lived a perfect life. Is it not logical and consistent, then, to believe that a true Christian will bear a definite resemblance to Christ, that the characteristics of the life of Christ will be revealed in him and will distinguish him from one who is not a Christian?

---

1   Ellen G. White, *Early Writings of Ellen G. White* (Washington D.C.: Review and Herald Publishing Association, 1945) 71.

Characteristics of the Pattern

We can think of many beautiful qualities of Christ, such as love, patience, kindness, purity, unselfishness, which all of us should possess and cultivate. But there was one pre-eminent characteristic, which was revealed in all His ministry above everything else. It is found in two texts:

"The Son of man is come to seek and to save that which was lost." (Luke 19:10)

"This is a faithful saying, and of all acceptation, that Christ Jesus came into the world to save sinners." (1 Timothy 1: 15)

The one great purpose of Christ in coming to this world was to save the lost. He lived among men, ministering to the poor and needy, healing the sick, casting out devils, cleansing the lepers, and setting the captives free. He finally went to the cross, bearing the sins of all humanity with the one great purpose of saving the lost.

We would consider it absurd for one to say, "I am a Christian, but I do not believe in Christ." Would it not be equally inconsistent to say, "I am a Christian, but I am not interested in saving the lost"? Such a person would be taking his stand on the side of Satan; for Jesus said, "He that is not with me is against me; and he that gathereth not with me scattereth abroad." (Matthew 12:30) If we are true Christians, we shall constantly seek to become more like our beloved Master, and the outstanding characteristic of our lives will be our passion for souls.

Following the Pattern

Jesus said, "Follow me, and I will make you fishers of men." Are you a fisher of men? If you reply, No, then you must admit that you are not following Christ. It is not a

101

matter of trying to win souls; it is a matter of following Christ. He is responsible for our success if we follow Him, but we need have no fear that He will fail on His part. What is He making? Fishers of men. If we are truly born again, re-created in the image of Christ, our likeness to Him will be demonstrated by our constant burden and our earnest, prayerful efforts to win souls more than in any other way. This was the experience of the Apostle Paul, who wrote:

> **"For though I be free from all men, yet have I made myself servant unto all, that I might gain the more. And unto the Jews I became as a Jew, that I might gain the Jews; to them that are under the law, as under the law, that I might gain them that are under the law; to them that are without law, as without law...that I might gain them that are without law. To the weak became I as weak, that I might gain the weak: I am made all things to all men, that I might by all means save some."** **(1 Corinthians 9:19–22)**

Six times in these four verses we hear that earnest, passionate longing to save the lost. This is one of the chief evidences of genuine conversion. As soon as Andrew realized that he had found the Messiah, he hastened away to find his brother, Peter, and brought him to Christ. (John 1:40–42) As soon as Philip accepted the invitation to follow the Master, he went after his friend Nathaniel and brought him to Christ. (John 1:43–46.) So it will always be.

An Impressive Lesson

One of Jesus' beautiful and important lessons, illustrating our relation to Him, is found in the Book of John:

> **"I am the true vine, and my Father is the husbandman. Every branch in me that beareth not fruit he taketh away: and every branch that beareth fruit, he purgeth**

it, that it may bring forth more fruit....Abide in me, and I in you. As the branch cannot bear fruit of itself, except it abide in the vine; no more can ye, except ye abide in me. I am the vine, ye are the branches: he that abideth in me, and I in him, the same bringeth forth much fruit: for without me ye can do nothing. If a man abide not in me, he is cast forth as a branch, and is withered; and men gather them, and cast them into the fire, and they are burned." (John 15:1, 2, 4–6)

Jesus is the vine, and we are the branches. We know that grapes grow on the branches, not on the vine, which brings us face to face with the important lesson that God's provision for the salvation of the lost is through the ministry of His people. If you and I and all the rest of God's children do not bear fruit, if we do not win souls, there will be no fruit. How can anyone who claims to be a child of God evade this solemn responsibility?

The next statement is an impressive one: "Every branch in me that beareth not fruit he taketh away." God provides branches for the bearing of fruit. If they bear no fruit, they are worthless, and He takes them away, for they are "cumberers of the ground." It is a serious thing to make an outward profession of Christianity, to go through the forms of religious worship year after year, yet bear no fruit. It is the life flowing from the living vine out into the branches that produces the fruit. If there is no fruit, it is evidence that the branch is not abiding in the vine. "He that abideth in me, and I in him, the same bringeth forth much fruit." This is the test of a genuine, living union with Christ. I know of no more solemn thought. It brings us face to face with God's plan in making us fishers of men.

Our Part in This Work

We recognize that when undertaking some work of importance, our success will largely depend upon our making the best possible preparation. It is not my intention to propose a theological course for those who aspire to become ministers, but to offer some simple suggestions for those who long to win a soul but do not know how to start. One of the first conditions is set forth in the words of the Apostle Paul:

"Study to shew thyself approved unto God, a workman that needeth not to be ashamed, rightly dividing the word of truth." **(2 Timothy 2:15)**

Here is a positive command to *study,* given by the One who created us, yet how lightly is it regarded! How can we expect to succeed if we neglect to study? It is the Word of God that we are to study. This Word is "quick, and powerful, and sharper than any two-edged sword." (Hebrews 4:12) As we present this Word, the Holy Spirit uses it to bring conviction to sinners and to lead them to repentance and conversion. Here is another helpful text regarding our preparation:

"Provide yourself with an outline of the sound teaching which you have heard from my lips, and be true to the faith and love which are in Christ Jesus." **(2 Timothy 1:13, Weymouth's Translation)**

Every Christian is commanded to study the doctrines which constitute the foundation of our faith and of God's message of salvation. It is important that we study and understand the new birth, baptism, the coming of Christ, the signs of the times, and other fundamental truths so that we shall be able to present them in a logical, attractive way. But that is not enough. We need to have an "outline" that will be clear and simple, and as far as possi-ble we should memorize it so as to be "ready always to give an answer to every man that asketh you a reason of the hope that is in you with meekness and fear." (1 Peter 3:15)

To those who are not familiar with God's message for these last days, it is impressive to meet one who knows what he believes, and who can turn to the Bible and read God's answers to their questions. They are interested when they meet a person, young or old, who declares frankly, "I do not hold any doctrine which I cannot prove from the Word of God."

Do Not Listen to Satan

Probably all who sincerely believe God's Word will agree, after studying these scriptures, that it is the Lord's purpose for every Christian to be a soul winner. We also need to understand that no one arouses the antagonism of Satan more than an earnest, enthusiastic fisher of men. We may expect, as we go to work determined not to give up until by the blessing of God we have won a soul, that the enemy will exert all his power to discourage and defeat us.

Someday the name of a person will come to your mind, and you will be impressed that you should make an effort to win him to Christ. But immediately another voice will tell you that the person would not be interested, or would resent your efforts, or that someone else would be received more favorably. Many excuses will be suggested why you should not follow the convictions of the Spirit of God. You would do well to remember that when the Holy Spirit suggests that you work for a soul, He is getting that soul prepared for your ministry.

Some years ago in a large college church I spoke on this subject, and in the afternoon a young man came to my room. He wanted to tell me about the most thrilling experience he had ever had. He said that while he was listening to the discourse, and I was emphasizing the necessity of responding at once when the Holy Spirit suggested someone to whom we should speak, it seemed as though a voice said to him, "You ought to speak to Mr. A. after the meeting."

He said that instantly another voice seemed to say, "Oh, no, it would do no good to talk to that fellow; he is the worst young man in this town. You know he was expelled from college just a short time ago." Then he said the first voice spoke again and said, "Yes, that is just the reason why you should try to help him. He is in great need." So the young man said that the argument was going on in his mind so intensely that he did not hear any more of the sermon. But he was impressed that he must do something.

As soon as the meeting closed, he reached over and touched Mr. A. on the shoulder and said, "Come on over in this little room." In a moment they were in the little room alone, and he said, "John, I have been thinking about you. I know you have had some trouble lately, but you know I had a lot of difficulties two years ago. Then I gave my heart to the Lord, and it made such a wonderful change; things have been going fine ever since. John, I was thinking about you and wishing that you would give your heart to the Lord and find the joy and peace you have never known."

He glanced up and saw tears running down John's cheeks. They talked it over, and kneeling down, John, with deep sorrow and penitence, confessed his sins and gave his heart to the Lord. And that young man, who had obeyed the voice of the Spirit and made this kindly appeal to John, told me there in my room that it was the most thrilling experience he had ever had, and he intended to make soul winning the great business of his life.

When I hear people say they would like to be soul winners, but they have to work hard and do not have time to make the necessary preparation, I think of the experience of Thomas A. Edison in producing the phonograph.

He worked on the machine for some time, improving it day by day until at last it repeated a word distinctly. With unlimited patience he toiled on, and at last the day came when it would repeat every word he spoke except the letter "S." Edison worked on that machine eighteen hours a day for seven months, or 3,780 hours to make it say "S," and it said "S." Many times since hearing of this experience, I have thought, "Oh, if those who claim to be children of God would put one half the earnestness and devotion and perseverance into the work of saving the lost, how quickly God's work might be finished and the saints be gathered home."

Knowledge Brings Responsibility

Another principle we need to consider in studying this subject of soul winning is our personal responsibility. The Apostle Paul wrote:

"For though I preach the gospel, I have nothing to glory of: for necessity is laid upon me; yea, woe is unto me, if I preach not the gospel." (1 Corinthians 9:16)

Many times I read this verse casually, thinking that it applied only to the great apostle. Then I suddenly awoke to the fact that this was not written in the Word of God for Paul any more than for me and for every other disciple of Christ. Knowledge of the gospel places upon you and me the solemn obligation to pass it on to others.

I have had many experiences which have impressed this truth deeply upon my heart. I once lived in a large city where I walked about a mile to my office every morning. On my way I passed a factory where a number of blind people were employed. I always watched them with interest as they made their way down the busy street to their shop.

I want you to imagine that one night there was a cloudburst in the mountains not far away, and a mighty torrent of water came rushing down the canyon and across the city, sweeping away the bridge which we crossed every morning. As I go to my work, I am startled to find the bridge gone and a raging river where there was usually but a small stream.

At once I think of the blind people and wonder whether they know that the bridge has been swept away. I look up and see them coming, and I feel very sorry for them because they are blind and cannot see their danger. As they come to the end of the walk and plunge over into the angry waters, I feel thankful to the Lord that I can see. Let me ask you, Could you possibly regard me as a Christian? Do you not think that God would hold me accountable for the lives of those blind people, just as surely as though I had murdered them? They were blind. I saw them approaching the river, unconscious that the bridge was gone, and I did nothing.

Suppose I had hastened out and taken a blind man by the arm, saying, "Wait a minute, friend, there has been a cloudburst in the mountains and the bridge has been washed away, so you cannot get across." He replies, "Please attend to your own business; I can take care of myself," and he passes on and plunges down to a watery grave. I stop the next one, and the next, with the same results. I pray God to help me save these people. Then a man listens to my warning; his face turns pale, and he cries out, "What, the bridge gone! Oh, I am so glad you told me. You have saved my life, and I shall never forget you." Do you not think it worth all the effort even to save one?

Someday We Shall Face the Record

I was in China and a terrible famine was raging; it was known as the "year of the great famine." It was said that 42,000,000 people were facing starvation. With a physician and two missionaries I went back in the interior into the heart of that famine-stricken territory. Nothing can ever erase from my mind those awful scenes of suffering, starvation, and death. All along the streets men, women, and children were lying. It was often difficult to distinguish the living from the dead. It is appalling to see thousands of human beings, just skin and bones, with a few rags wrapped around them, lying in the streets with no help. The stench of decaying corpses was beyond description.

We went to one section of the city where 12,500 women and children occupied a compound surrounded by a high wall. Across the road about half as many men were in another enclosure. Just imagine that you were there with us, and that we had possession of a vast building, filled with hundreds of carloads of grains, vegetables, and other foods. We talk matters over and decide that since we do not know how long the famine may last, the wise course will be to keep the storehouse securely locked and guarded so that none of the supplies can be taken. All around that great building the emaciated bodies of human beings are lying, some moaning and pleading for help, while others die in silence. Would you pursue such a course as that? I know you would not, for you would realize that God would hold you responsible for saving the lives of as many as possible while the food lasted. Does not this illustrate what the Apostle Paul had in mind? You and I have the light of God's message for these last days. We have studied the prophecies concerning Christ's coming and have seen them fulfilled, and we know that our time to witness for Him is short. All around us are thousands who are perishing for the bread of life. We have an inexhaustible supply. We need not fear to give away the living bread, for the more we give, the more our divine Master will give to us. God has entrusted to us the last appeal to a doomed world. Though we preach the gospel, we have nothing to glory of, for necessity is laid upon us: yea, woe is unto us if we preach not the gospel.

Jesus says to us today, "Follow me, and I will make you fishers of men." What other ambition in this world is of importance compared with the work of saving the lost? We want to be saved and have a home in the mansions above. One of the greatest joys of the redeemed through eternal ages will be found in associating with the souls to whom it was our privilege to bring the light and knowledge of our Redeemer.

So the Master says, "Go your ways: behold, I send you forth as lambs among wolves." What a thrilling commission! Noble, innocent lambs going bravely out into the enemy's territory among the fierce, ugly wolves, but surrounded with such an atmosphere of love, sympathy, and unselfish interest that the barriers melt away, and the wolves let us introduce them to Jesus, who transforms them into lambs. Someday soon He will gather all the lambs into the heavenly fold to share its joys forever.

"It is not the one who knows the most; nor the one who says the most; nor the one who does the most; but the one who loves the most, who wins the most."

May God help us to keep our eyes on the supreme goal.

We invite you to view the complete
selection of titles we publish at:
www.TEACHServices.com

scan with your mobile
device to go directly
to our website

Please write or email us your praises, reactions, or
thoughts about this or any other book we publish at:

TEACH Services, Inc.
P U B L I S H I N G
www.TEACHServices.com ● (800) 367-1844

Info@TEACHServices.com

TEACH Services, Inc., titles may be purchased in bulk
for educational, business, fund-raising, or sales
promotional use. For information, please e-mail:

BulkSales@TEACHServices.com

Finally if you are interested in seeing
your own book in print, please contact us at

publishing@TEACHServices.com

We would be happy to review your manuscript for free.